3-

SELECTED & NEW POEMS

1961–1981

BOOKS BY JIM HARRISON

SELECTED & NEW POEMS

1961–1981

Jim Harrison

Drawings by
Russell Chatham

DELACORTE PRESS/SEYMOUR LAWRENCE

Published by
Delacorte Press/Seymour Lawrence
1 Dag Hammarskjold Plaza
New York, N.Y. 10017

Some of the poems in this book first appeared in the books PLAIN
SONG, Copyright © 1965 by James Harrison, W. W. Norton & Co. Inc.;
LOCATIONS, Copyright © 1968 by James Harrison, W. W. Norton &
Co. Inc.; OUTLYER AND GHAZALS, Copyright © 1969, 1971 by Jim
Harrison, Simon & Schuster; and LETTERS TO YESENIN, Copyright ©
1973 by Jim Harrison, Sumac Press.

Manufactured in the United States of America

First printing

Designed by MaryJane DiMassi

LIBRARY OF CONGRESS CATALOGING IN PUBLICATION DATA

Harrison, Jim, 1937–
Selected & new poems, 1961–1981.

I. Title.   II. Title: Selected and new poems, 1961–1981.
PS3558.A67A6   1982   811'.54   81–19494
ISBN 0–440–07994–2   AACR2
ISBN 0–440–08002–9 (signed and limited edition)
ISBN 0–440–58048–X (pbk.)

to John and Rebecca

from

PLAIN SONG

POEM

Form is the woods: the beast,
a bobcat padding through red sumac,
the pheasant in brake or goldenrod
that he stalks—both rise to the flush,
the brief low flutter and catch in air;
and trees, rich green, the moving of boughs
and the separate leaf, yield
to conclusions they do not care about
or watch—the dead, frayed bird,
the beautiful plumage,
the spoor of feathers
and slight, pink bones.

SKETCH FOR A
JOB APPLICATION BLANK

My left eye is blind and jogs like
a milky sparrow in its socket;
my nose is large and never flares
in anger, the front teeth, bucked,
but not in lechery—I sucked
my thumb until the age of twelve.
O my youth was happy and I was never lonely
though my friends called me "pig eye"
and the teachers thought me loony.

>   (When I bruised, my psyche kept intact:
>   I fell from horses, and once a cow but never
>   pigs—a neighbor lost a hand to a sow.)

But I had some fears:
the salesman of eyes,
his case was full of fishy baubles,
against black velvet, jeweled gore,
the great cocked hoof of a Belgian mare,
a nest of milk snakes by the water trough,
electric fences,
my uncle's hounds,
the pump arm of an oil well,
the chop and whirr of a combine in the sun.

From my ancestors, the Swedes,
I suppose I inherit the love of rainy woods,
kegs of herring and neat whiskey—
I remember long nights of pinochle,
the bulge of Redman in my grandpa's cheek;
the rug smelled of manure and kerosene.
They laughed loudly and didn't speak for days.

>   (But on the other side, from the German Mennonites,
>   their rag smoke prayers and porky daughters
>   I got intolerance, an aimless diligence.)

In '51 during a revival I was saved:
I prayed on a cold register for hours

and woke up lame. I was baptized
by immersion in the tank at Williamston—
the rusty water stung my eyes.
I left off the old things of the flesh
but not for long—one night beside a pond
she dried my feet with her yellow hair.
      O actual event dead quotient
      cross become green
I still love Jubal but pity Hagar.

     (Now self is the first sacrament
     who loves not the misery and taint
     of the present tense is lost.
     I strain for a lunar arrogance.
             Light macerates
             the lamp infects
   warmth, more warmth, I cry.)

DAVID

He is young. The father is dead.
Outside, a cold November night,
the mourner's cars are parked upon the lawn;
beneath the porch light three
brothers talk to three sons
and shiver without knowing it.
His mind's all black thickets
and blood; he knows
flesh slips quietly off the bone,
he knows no last looks,
that among the profusion of flowers
the lid is closed to hide
what no one could bear—
that metal rends the flesh,
he knows beneath the white pointed
creatures, stars,
that in the distant talk of brothers,
the father is dead.

EXERCISE

Hear this touch: grass parts
for the snake,
in furrows
soil curves around itself,
a rock topples into a lake,
roused organs,
fur against cloth,
arms unfold,
at the edge of a clearing
fire selects new wood.

A SEQUENCE OF WOMEN

I

I've known her too long:
we devour as two mirrors,
opposed,
swallow each other a thousand
times at midpoints,
lost in the black center
of the other.

II

She sits on the bed,
breasts slack,
watching a curl of dust
float through a ray of sun,
drift down to a corner.
So brief this meeting
with a strange child—
Do I want to be remembered?
Only as a mare might know
the body of her rider,
the pressure of legs
unlike any other.

III

The girl who was once my mistress
is dead now, I learn, in childbirth.
I thought that long ago women ceased
dying this way.

To set records straight, our enmity
relaxes, I wrote a verse for her—
to dole her by pieces, ring finger
and lock of hair.

But I'm a poor Midas to turn her golden,
to make a Helen, grand whore, of this graceless
girl; the sparrow that died was only
a sparrow:

Though in the dark, she doesn't sleep.
On cushions, embraced by silk, no lover
comes to her. In the first light when birds
stir she does not stir or sing. Oh eyes can't
focus to this dark.

NORTHERN MICHIGAN

On this back road the land
has the juice taken out of it:

stump fences surround nothing
worth their tearing down

by a deserted filling station
a Veedol sign, the rusted hulk

of a Frazer, "live bait"
on battered tin.

                    A barn
with half a tobacco ad
owns the greenness of a manure
pile

a half moon on a privy door
a rope swinging from an elm. A

collapsed hen house, a pump
with the handle up

the orchard with wild tangled branches.

. . . .

In the far corner of the pasture,
in the shadow of the wood lot
a herd of twenty deer:
                    three bucks
are showing off—
they jump in turn across the fence,
flanks arch and twist to get higher
in the twilight
as the last light filters
through the woods.

FAIR/BOY CHRISTIAN
TAKES A BREAK

This other speaks of bones, blood-wet
and limber, the rock in bodies. He takes
me to the slaughter house, where lying
sprawled, as a giant coil of rope,
the bowels of cattle. At the county fair
we pay an extra quarter to see the her-
maphrodite. We watch the secret air tube
blow up the skirts of the farm girls,
tanned to the knees then strangely white.
We eat spareribs and pickled eggs,
the horses tear the ground to pull a load
of stone; in a burning tent we see
Fantasia do her Love Dance with the
Spaniard—they glisten with sweat, their
limbs knot together while below them farm
boys twitter like birds. Then the breasts
of a huge Negress rotate to a march in
opposing directions, and everyone stamps
and cheers, the udders shine in blurring
speed. Out of the tent we pass produce
stalls, some hung with ribbons, squash
and potatoes stacked in pyramids. A buck-
toothed girl cuts her honorable mention
cake; when she leans to get me water
from a milk pail her breasts are chaste.
Through the evening I sit in the car (the
other is gone) while my father watches
the harness race, the 4-H talent show.
I think of St. Paul's Epistles and pray
the removal of what my troubled eyes have seen.

MORNING

The mirror tastes him
breath clouds
hands pressed against glass

in yellow morning light
a jay
flutters in unaccustomed
silence
from bush to limb of elm

a cow at breakfast
pauses
her jaws lax in momentary stillness

far off a milk truck
rattles
on the section road

light low mist
floats
over the buckwheat
through the orchard

the neighbor's dogs bark
then four roosters announce
day.

KINSHIP

Great-uncle Wilhelm, Mennonite, patriarch,
eater of blood sausage, leeks,
head cheese, salt pork,
you are led into church
by that wisp you plundered for nine children.
Your brain has sugared now,
your white beard is limp,
you talk of acres of corn
where there is only snow.
Your sister, a witch, old as a stump
says you are punished now for the unspeakable
sin that barred you from the table for seven years.
They feed you cake to hasten your death.
Your land is divided.
Curse them but don't die.

FEBRUARY SUITE

Song,
angry bush
with the thrust of your roots
deep in this icy ground,
is there a polar sun?

. . . .

Month of the frozen
goat—
La Roberta says cultivate
new friends,
                profit will
be yours with patience.
Not that stars are crossed
or light to be restored—
we die from want of velocity.

And you, longest of months
with your false springs,
you don't help or care about helping,
so splendidly ignorant of us.
Today icicles fell
but they will build downwards again.

. . . .

Who has a "fate"?
This fig tree
talks
about bad weather.

. . . .

Here is man drunk—
in the glass
his blurred innocence renewed.

. . . .

The Great Leitzel
before falling to her death
did 249 flanges on the Roman rings—
her wrist was often raw
and bloody
but she kept it hidden.

. . . .

He remembers Memorial Day—
the mother's hymn to Generals.
The American Legion fires blanks
out over the lassitude of the cemetery
in memory of sons who broke
like lightbulbs in a hoarse cry
of dust.

. . . .

Now
behind bone
in the perfect dark
the dreams of animals.

. . . .

To remember
the soft bellies of fish
the furred animals that were part of your youth
not for their novelty
but as fellow creatures.

. . . .

I look at the rifles
in their rack upon the wall:
though I know the Wars
only as history
some cellar in Europe might still
owe some of its moistness to blood.

. . . .

With my head on the table
I write,

my arm outstretched, in another field,
of richer grain.

. . . .

A red-haired doll stares
at me from a highchair,
her small pink limbs twisted about
her neck.
I salute the postures of women.

. . . .

This hammer of joy,
this is no fist
but a wonderment got by cunning.

The first thunderstorm
of March came last night
and when I awoke the snow had passed
away, the brown grass
lay matted and pubic.

Between the snow and grass,
somewhere into the ground with the rain
a long year has gone.

REVERIE

He thinks of the dead. But they
appear as dead—beef colored and torn.

There is a great dull music
in the ocean that lapses into seascape.

The girl bends slowly
from the waist. Then stoops.

In high school Brutus
died upon a rubber knife.

Lift the smock. The sun
light stripes her back. A *fado* wails.

In an alley in Cambridge. Beneath
a party's noise. Bottle caps stuck to them.

NIGHTMARE

Through the blinds
a white arm caresses a vase of zinnias

beneath the skin
of a pond the laughter of an eye

in the loft
the hot straw suffocates
the rafters become snakes

through the mow door
three deer in a cool pasture
nibbling at the grass
mercurous in the moon.

[16]

DUSK

Dusk over the lake,
clouds floating
heat lightning
a nightmare behind branches;
from the swamp
the odor of cedar and fern,
the long circular
wail of the loon—
the plump bird aches for fish
for night to come down.

Then it becomes so dark
and still
that I shatter the moon with an oar.

LISLE'S RIVER

Dust followed our car like a dry brown cloud.
At the river we swam, then in the canoe passed
downstream toward Manton; the current carried us
through cedar swamps, hot fields of marsh grass
where deer watched us and the kildeer shrieked.
We were at home in a thing that passes.
And that night, camped on a bluff, we ate eggs
and ham and three small trout; we drank too much
whiskey and pushed a burning stump down the bank—
it cast hurling shadows, leaves silvered and darkened,
the crash and hiss woke up a thousand birds.

Now, tell me, other than lying between some woman's legs,
what joy have you had since that equaled this?

THREE NIGHT SONGS

I

He waits to happen with the clear
reality of what he thinks about—
to be a child that wakes beautifully,
a man always in the state of waking
to a new room, or at night, waking
to a strange room with snow outside,
and the moon beyond glass,
in a net of branches,
so bright and clear and cold.

II

Moving in liquid dark,
night's water,
a flat stone sinking,
wobbling toward bottom;
and not to wait there for morning,
to see the sun up through the water,
but to freeze until another glacier comes.

III

The mask riddles itself,
there's heat through the eye slits,
a noise of breathing,
the plaster around the mouth is wet;
and the dark takes no effort,
dark against deeper dark,
the mask dissembled,
a music comes to the point of horror.

JOHN SEVERIN WALGREN,
1874–1962

Trees die of thirst or cold
or when the limit's reached;
in the hole in the elm
the wood is soft and punky—
it smells of the water of a vase
after the flowers are dumped.

You were so old we could not weep;
only the blood of the young,
those torn off earth in a night's sickness,
the daughter lying beside you
who became nothing so long ago—
she moves us to terror.

MALEDICTION

Man's not a singing animal,
his tongue hangs from a wall—
        pinch the stone
        to make a moan
        from the throat
        a single note
        breaks the air
        so bare and harsh
        birds die.

He's crab-necked from cold,
song splits his voice
like a lake's ice cracking.
His heart's a rock,
a metronome, a clock,
a foghorn drone of murder.

God, curse this self-maimed beast,
the least of creatures, rivet his stone with worms.

YOUNG BULL

The bronze ring punctures
the flesh of your nose,
the wound is fresh
and you nuzzle the itch
against a fence post.
Your testicles are fat and heavy
and sway when you shake off flies;
the chickens scratch about your feet
but you do not notice them.

Through lunch I pitied
you from the kitchen window—
the heat, pained fluid of August—
but when I came with cold water
and feed, you bellowed and heaved
against the slats wanting to murder me.

PARK AT NIGHT

Unwearied
the coo and choke
of doves
the march of stone
an hour before dawn.

Trees caged to the waist
wet statues
the trickling of water—
in the fountain
floating across the lamp
a leaf
some cellophane.

HITCHHIKING

Awake:
the white hand of
my benefactor
drums on the seat
between us.
The world had become orange
in the rear view mirror
of a fifty-five Pontiac.
The road was covered with bugs
and mist coiled around
great house-sized rocks
and in the distance buried them.
Village. Passed three limp
gas stations then one
whose windows exploded with fire.
My mouth was filled with plastic cups.
Final item:
breakfast, nurtured
by a miraculous hatred.

SOUND

At dawn I squat on the garage
with snuff under a lip
to sweeten the roofing nails—
my shoes and pant cuffs
are wet with dew.
In the orchard the peach trees
sway with the loud
weight of birds, green fruit, yellow haze.
And my hammer—the cold head taps,
then swings its first full arc;
the sound echoes against the barn,
muffled in the loft,
and out the other side, then lost
in the noise of the birds
as they burst from the trees.

LI HO

Li Ho of the province of Honan
        (not to be confused with the god Li Po
        of Kansu or Szechuan
        who made twenty thousand verses)
Li Ho, whose mother said
"my son daily vomits up his heart"
mounts his horse and rides
to where a temple lies as lace among foliage.
His youth is bargained
for some poems in his saddlebag—
his beard is gray. Leaning
against the flank of his horse he considers
the flight of birds
but his hands are heavy. (Take this cup,
he thinks, fill it, I want to drink again.)
Deep in his throat, but perhaps it is a bird,
he hears a child cry.

DEAD DEER

Amid pale green milkweed, wild clover,
a rotted deer
curled, shaglike,
after a winter so cold
the trees split open.
I think she couldn't keep up with
the others (they had no place
to go) and her food,
frozen grass and twigs,
wouldn't carry her weight.

Now from bony sockets,
she stares out on this
cruel luxuriance.

from

LOCATIONS

WALKING

Walking back on a chill morning past Kilmer's Lake
into the first broad gully, down its trough
and over a ridge of poplar, scrub oak, and into
a larger gully, walking into the slow fresh warmth
of midmorning to Spider Lake where I drank
at a small spring remembered from ten years back;
walking northwest two miles where another gully
opened, seeing a stump on a knoll where my father
stood one deer season, and tiring of sleet and cold
burned a pine stump, the snow gathering fire-orange
on a dull day; walking past charred stumps blackened
by the '81 fire to a great hollow stump near a basswood
swale—I sat within it on a November morning
watching deer browse beyond my young range of shotgun
and slug, chest beating hard for killing—
into the edge of a swale waist high with ferns,
seeing the quick movement of a blue racer,
and thick curl of the snake against a birch log,
a pale blue with nothing of the sky in it,
a fleshy blue, blue of knotted veins in an arm;
walking to Savage's Lake where I ate my bread
and cheese, drank cool lake water, and slept for a while,
dreaming of fire, snake and fish and women in white
linen walking, pinkish warm limbs beneath white linen;
then waking, walking homeward toward Well's Lake,
brain at boil now with heat, afternoon glistening
in yellow heat, dead dun-brown grass, windless,
with all distant things shimmering, grasshoppers, birds
dulled to quietness; walking a log road near a cedar swamp
looking cool with green darkness and whine of mosquitoes,
crow's caw overhead, Cooper's hawk floating singly
in mateless haze; walking dumbly, footsore, cutting
into evening through sumac and blackberry brambles,
onto the lake road, feet sliding in the gravel,
whippoorwills, night birds wakening, stumbling to lake
shore, shedding clothes on sweet moss; walking
into syrupy August moonless dark, water cold, pushing

lily pads aside, walking out into the lake with feet
springing on mucky bottom until the water flows overhead;
sinking again to walk on the bottom then buoyed up,
walking on the surface, moving through beds of reeds,
snakes and frogs moving, to the far edge of the lake
then walking upward over the basswood and alders, the field
of sharp stubble and hay bales, toward the woods,
floating over the bushy crests of hardwoods and tips
of pine, barely touching in miles of rolling heavy dark,
coming to the larger water, there walking along the troughs
of waves folding in upon themselves; walking to an island,
small, narrow, sandy, sparsely wooded, in the middle
of the island in a clump of cedars a small spring
which I enter, sliding far down into a deep cool
dark endless weight of water.

SUITE TO FATHERS

For D.I.

I

I think that night's our balance,
our counterweight—a blind woman
we turn to for nothing but dark.

* * *

In Val-Mont I see a slab of parchment
a black quill pen in stone.
In a sculptor's garden
there was a head made from stone,
large as a room, the eyes neatly hooded
staring out with a crazed somnolence
fond of walled gardens.

* * *

The countesses arch like cats in châteaux.
They wake up as countesses and usually sleep with counts.
Nevertheless he writes them painful letters,
thinking of Eleanor of Aquitaine, Gaspara Stampa.
With Kappus he calls forth the stone in the rose.

* * *

In Egypt the dhows sweep the Nile
with ancient sails. I am in Egypt,
he thinks, this Baltic jew—it is hot,
how can I make bricks with no straw?
His own country rich with her food and slaughter,
fit only for sheep and generals.

* * *

He thinks of the coffin of the East,
of the tiers of dead in Venice,
those countless singulars.
At lunch, the baked apple too sweet with kirsche
becomes the tongues of convent girls at gossip,
under the drum and shadow of pigeons
the girl at promenade has almond in her hair.

* * *

From Duino, beneath the mist,
the green is so dark and green it cannot bear itself.
In the night, from black paper
I cut the silhouette of this exiled god,
finding him as the bones of a fish in stone.

II

In the cemetery the grass is pale,
fake green as if dumped from Easter baskets,
from overturned clay and the deeper marl
which sits in wet gray heaps by the creek.
There are no frogs, death drains there.
Landscape of glass, perhaps Christ
will quarry you after the worms.
The newspaper says caskets float in leaky vaults.
Above me, I feel paper birds.
The sun is a brass bell.
This is not earth I walk across
but the pages of some giant magazine.

* * *

Come song,
allow me some eloquence,
good people die.

* * *

The June after you died
I dove down into a lake,

the water turned to cold, then colder,
and ached against my ears.
I swam under a sunken log then paused,
letting my back rub against it,
like some huge fish with rib cage
and soft belly open to the bottom.
I saw the light shimmering far above
but did not want to rise.

* * *

It was so far up from the dark—
once it was night three days,
after that four, then six and over again.
The nest was torn from the tree,
the tree from the ground,
the ground itself sinking torn.
I envied the dead their sleep of rot.
I was a fable to myself,
a speech to become meat.

III

Once in Nevada I sat on a boulder at twilight—
I had no ride and wanted to avoid the snakes.
I watched the full moon rise a fleshy red
out of the mountains, out of a distant sand storm.
I thought then if I might travel deep enough
I might embrace the dead as equals,
not in their separate stillnesses as dead, but in music
one with another's harmonies.
The moon became paler,
rising, floating upwards in her arc
and I with her, intermingled in her whiteness,
until at dawn again she bloodied
herself with earth.

* * *

In the beginning I trusted in spirits,
slight things, those of the dead in procession,

the household gods in mild delirium
with their sweet round music and modest feasts.
Now I listen only to that hard black core,
a ball harsh as coal, rending for light
far back in my own sour brain.

* * *

The tongue knots itself
a cramped fist of music,
the oracle a white-walled room of bone
which darkens now with a greater dark;
and the brain a glacier of blood,
inching forward, sliding, the bottom
silt covered but sweet,
becoming a river now
laving the skull with coolness—
the leaves on her surface
dipping against the bone.

* * *

Voyager, the self the voyage—
dark let me open your lids.
Night stares down with her great bruised eye.

SUITE TO APPLENESS

I

If you love me drink this discolored wine,
tanning at the edge with the sourness of flowers—
their heads, soldiers', floating as flowers,
heads, necks, owned by gravity now as war
owned them and made them move to law;
and the water is heavier than war, the heads
bobbing freely there with each new wave lap.

* * *

And if your arm offends you, cut it off.
Then the leg by walking, tear out the eye,
the trunk, body be eyeless, armless, bodiless.
And if your brain offends you . . .
If Christ offends you tear him out,
or if the earth offends you, skin her
back in rolls, nailed to dry
on barnside, an animal skin in sunlight;
or the earth that girl's head,
throwing herself from the asylum roof,
head and earth whirling earthwards.

* * *

Or if we reoccur with death our humus, heat,
as growths or even mushrooms; on my belly
I sight for them at dead-leaf line—
no better way—thinking there that I hear
the incredible itch of things to grow,
Spring, soon to be billion-jetted.

* * *

Earth in the boy's hand, the girl's head,
standing against the granary; earth a green

apple he picked to throw at starlings,
plucked from among green underleaves,
silver leaf bellies burred with fine white hairs;
the apple hurled, hurtling greenly with wet solidity,
earth spinning in upon herself,
shedding her brains and whales and oceans,
her mountains strewn and crushed.

II

In the Quonset shed unloading the fertilizer,
each bag weighing eighty pounds,
muscles ache, lungs choke with heat and nitrogen;
then climbing the ladder of the water tank
to see in the orchard the brightness of apples,
sinking clothed into the icy water, feet thunking
iron bottom, a circle of hot yellow light above.

* * *

The old tree, a McIntosh:
68 bushel last year,
with 73 bushel the year before that,
sitting up within it on a smooth branch,
avoiding the hoe, invisible to the ground,
buoyed up by apples, brain still shocked,
warped, shaved into curls of paper,
a wasps' globe of gray paper—
lamina of oil and clouds—
now drawing in greenness, the apples
swelling to heaviness on a hot August afternoon;
to sing, singing, voice cracks at second sing,
paper throat, brain unmoist for singing.

* * *

Cranking the pump to loud life,
the wheel three turns to the left,
six hundred feet of pipe laying in the field;
the ground beneath begins shaking, bumping

with the force of coming water, sprinklers whirl,
the ground darkening with spray of flung water.

* * *

After the harvest of cabbage the cabbage roots,
an acre of them and the discarded outer leaves,
scaly pale green roots against black soil,
to be forked into piles with the tomato vines;
a warm week later throwing them onto the wagon,
inside the piles the vines and leaves have rotted,
losing shape, into a thick green slime and jelly.

III

Or in the orchard that night
in July: the apple trees too thick
with branches, unpruned, abandoned,
to bear good fruit—the limbs
moving slightly in still air with my drunkenness;
a cloud passed over the moon
sweeping the orchard with a shadow—
the shadow moving thickly across the darkening field,
a moving lustrous dark, toward a darker wood lot.

* * *

Then the night exploded with crows—
an owl or raccoon disturbed a nest—
I saw them far off above the trees,
small pieces of black in the moonlight
in shrill fury circling with caw caw caw,
skin prickling with its rawness
brain swirling with their circling
in recoil moving backward, crushing
the fallen apples with my feet,
the field moving then as the folds
of a body with their caw caw caw.
Young crows opened by owl's beak,
raccoon's claws and teeth,

night opened, brain broken as with a hammer
by weight of blackness and crows,
crushed apples and drunkenness.

* * *

Or Christ bless torn Christ, crows,
the lives of their young
torn from the darkness,
apples and the dead webbed branches
choking the fruit;
night and earth herself
a drunken hammer, the girl's head,
all things bruised or crushed
as an apple.

THE SIGN

There are no magic numbers or magic lives.
He dreams of Sagittarius in a thicket,
dogs yipe at his hoofs, the eye of the archer
seaward, his gaze toward impossible things—
bird to be fish, archer and horse a whale
or dolphin; then rears up, canters
away from the shore across a wide field
of fern and honeysuckle brambles
to a woods where he nibbles at small
fresh leeks coming up among dead leaves.

* * *

Strange creature to be thought of,
welded in the skull as unicorn,
hoofs, bow, quiver of arrows and beard;
that girl sitting at cliff edge
or beside a brook, how does he take her?
He lifts her up to kiss her,
and at night standing by a stream,
heavy mist up to his flanks,
mist curling and floating through his legs,
a chill comes over him;
she in restless sleep in a small stone cottage.

* * *

Between the scorpion and goat,
three signs—
winter in cancer and this love of snow.

* * *

And contempt for all signs, the nine
spokes of the sun, the imagined belt

of dark or girdle in which night
mantles herself. The stars guide
no one save those at sea
or in the wilderness; avoid what stinks
or causes pain, hate death and cruelty
to any living thing.
You do not need the stars for that.

II

But often at night something asks
the brain to ride, run riderless;
plumed night swirling, brain riding itself
through blackness, crazed with motion,
footless against the earth,
perhaps hoofs imagined in lunacy;
through swamps feared even in daytime
at gallop, crashing through poplar
thickets, tamarack, pools of green slime,
withers splattered with mud, breathing
deep in an open marsh in the center of
the great swamp, then running again
toward a knoll of cedar where deer feed,
pausing, stringing the bow, chasing
the deer for miles, crossing a black-top road
where the hoofs clatter.

* * *

On a May night walking home from a tavern
through a village with only three streetlights,
a slip of moon and still air moist with scent of first grass;
to look into the blackness by the roadside,
and in all directions, village, forest
and field covered with it:
        eighteen miles of black to Traverse City
        thirteen miles of black to Buckley
        nineteen miles of black to Karlin
        twelve miles of black to Walton Junction

* * *

[42]

And infinite black above;
earth herself a heavy whirling ball of pitch.
If the brain expands to cover these distances . . .
stumbling to the porch where the cat
has left an injured snake that hisses with the brain,
the brain rearing up to shed the black
and the snake coiled bleeding at its center

III

Not centaur or archer but man,
man standing exhausted at night
beneath a night sky so deep and measureless,
head thrown back he sees his constellation,
his brain fleshes it and draws the lines
which begin to ripple then glimmer,
heave and twist, assume color, rear up,
the head high, the chest and torso gleaming,
beard glistening, flanks strapped with muscle,
hoofs stomping in place, stomping night's floor,
rearing again, fading, then regaining terror,
the bow in hand, a strung bow, and arrow fitted,
drawn back, the arrow molten tipped.
Slay. He only still "slays."
And when the arrow reaches earth I'll die.

* * *

But in morning light, already shrill and hot
by ten, digging a well pit, the sandy earth crumbles
and traps the legs, binding them to earth; then digging
again, driving a shallow well with a sledge,
the well tip shaped as an arrow head, sledge hitting
steel with metallic ring and scream; the pump head
and arm bound to pipe, sitting in damp sand
with legs around the pipe pumping the first water
onto my chest and head—head swollen with pain
of last night's sign and leavings of whiskey.

* * *

On another morning, the frost as a sheet
of white stubbled silk soon to melt into greenness,
partridge thumping ground with wings to call their mates,
near a river, thick and turbulent and brown—
a great buck deer, startled
from a thicket, a stag of a thousand stories,
how easily his spread antlers trace a back and bow
not unlike your own, then the arc of him
bounding away into his green clear music.

WAR SUITE

I

The wars: we're drawn to them
as if in fever, we sleepwalk to them,
wake up in full stride of nightmare,
blood slippery, mouth deep in their gore.

* * *

Even in Gilgamesh, the darker bodies
strewn over stone battlements,
dry skin against rough stone, the sand
sifting through rock face, swollen flesh
covered with it, sand against blackening lips,
flesh covered with it, the bodies
bloating in the heat, then hidden,
then covered; or at an oasis, beneath
still palms, a viper floats toward water,
her soft belly flattened of its weight, tongue
flicking at water beside the faces of the dead,
their faces, chests, pressed to earth, bodies
also flattened, lax with their weight,
now surely groundlings, and the moon
swollen in the night, the sheen
of it on lax bodies and on the water.

* * *

Now in Aquitaine, this man is no less dead
for being noble, a knight with a clang
and rasp to his shield and hammer;
air thick with horses,
earth fixed under their moving feet
but bodies falling, sweat and blood
under armor, death blows, sweet knight's
blood flowing, horses screaming, horses
now riderless drinking at a brook, mouths sore

with bits, sweat drying gray on flanks,
noses dripping cool water, nibbling
grass through bits, patches of grass
with the blood still red and wet on them.

II

I sing sixty-seven wars; the war now,
the war for Rapunzel, earth cannot use
her hair, the war of drowning hair
drifting upward as it descends,
the lover holding his cock like
a switch-blade, war of
apples and pears beating against the earth,
earth tearing a hole in sky, air to hold
the light it has gathered, river bending
until its back is broken, death a black
carp to swim in our innards.

* * *

Grand wars; the final auk poised
on her ice floe, the wolf shot
from a helicopter; that shrill god
in her choir loft among damp wine-colored
crumpled robes, face against a dusty
window, staring out at a black pond
and the floor of a wood lot
covered with ferns—if that wasp
on the pane stings her . . .
cancer to kill child, child to kill cancer,
nail to enter the wood, the Virgin
to flutter in the air above Rome like a Piper Cub,
giraffe's neck to grow after greener leaves,
bullet to enter an eye, bullet
to escape the skull, bullet to fall
to earth, eye to look for its skull,
skull to burst, belly to find its cage or ribs.

* * *

Face down in the pool, his great fatty
heart wants to keep beating; tongue pressed
to rug in a chemical hallway; on a country
road, caught by flashbulb headlights,
he wishes suddenly to be stronger than a car.

III

The elephant to couple in peace,
the porpoise to be free of the microphone;
this page to know a master, a future,
a page with the flesh melodious,
to bring her up through the page, paper shrouded,
from whatever depth she lies,
dulling her gift, bringing her to song
and not to life.

* * *

This death mask to harden before
the face escapes, life passes
down through the neck—the sculptor
turns hearing it rub against the door.

* * *

Mind to stay free of madness, of war;
war all howling and stiff-necked dead,
night of mind punctuated with moans and stars,
black smoke moiling, puling mind striped as a zebra,
ass in air madly stalking her lion.

* * *

Fire to eat tar, tar to drip,
hare to beat hound
grouse to avoid shot
trout to shake fly
chest to draw breath
breath to force song,

a song to be heard,
remembered and sung.

* * *

To come to an opening in a field
without pausing, to move there in a full circle of light;
but night's out there not even behind the glass—
there's nothing to keep her out or in;
to walk backwards to her, to step
off her edge or become her edge,
to swell and roll in her darkness,
a landlocked sea moving free
dark and clear within her continent.

AMERICAN GIRL

I

Not a new poem for Helen,
if they were heaped . . .
but she never wanted a poem,
an aimless altogether wanton pussy
whose affections the moment aimed.
And not to sing a new Helen into being
with t'adores, anachronistic gymnastics,
to be diligent in praise of her
only to be struck down by her.
Sing then, if song,
after bitter retreat,
on your knees,
as anyone who would love.
My senses led me here
and I had no wit to do otherwise.
Who breathes. Has looked upon. Alone.
In the darkness. Remembers.

* * *

Better to sit as a boy did in a still
cool attic in fall, tomatoes left to ripen
in autumn light on newspapers,
sucking his honeyed thumb, the forbidden
magazine across the lap and only
the mind's own nakedness for company;
the lovely photo, almost damp,
as supple and pink to the eye,
a hot country of body
but unknown and distant,
perhaps futureless.

* * *

A child once thought the dead were buried
to bear children: in the morning from his loft
in the fumes of wood smoke and bacon
he watches them dress, their bathing suits drying
by the stove. The water will fill them up.

II

He dreams of Egypt in Sunday School,
the maidens of Ur-of-Chaldea, Bathsheba bathing
on her rooftop, the young virgin brought
to David to warm his hollow bones. And the horror
of Sodom and Gomorrah, Lot's frenzy
with his daughters; women railed against
in Habakkuk and Jeremiah, Isaiah's feverish
wife and Christ and the woman at the well—
to look in lust is to do without doing;
eyes follow the teacher's rump as she leaves the room.

* * *

At sixteen his first whore, youngish
and acrid, sharing with her a yellow room
and a fifth of blackberry brandy;
first frightened with only his shoes on,
then calmed, then pleased, speechlessly
preening and arrogant. They became
blackberry brandy but never sweetly again—
vile in Laramie before dawn through
a darkened bar and up the long backstairs,
on Commerce St. in Grand Rapids shrieking
with gin. He craved some distant cousin
in Sweden he'd never seen, incestuously,
in some flower-strewn woods near the water.

* * *

After a New Year's and his first french meal,
enchanté of course pursing her thick lips,
throwing one leg over the other
in the abandonment of sitting down,

throwing off room-length heat beneath layers
of nylon, stuffed with turbot and filet as she is,
splendidly in health, though her only apparent
exercise is screwing, "making the love,"
not gentle like but as a Mack truck
noses a loading platform.

III

The same "she" seen from a bus
or store window, often too young,
across the subway tracks in pure ozone,
the blonde cheerleader with legs
bared to hundreds of eyes.
Always a fool before the coins—
I Ching forcing turmoil, the cauldron.
The fool has eyes and touch,
is mammalian. He lacks all odds,
ruts then is scathed. There's Helen
in a Greek nightclub, a hundred
years old and selling pistachios
half a century away from any bed—
her face a shucked pecan.

* * *

Near the shore in a bed of reeds
he finally sees her for a moment,
the moon their only witness,
a single white eye;
her face is swirling in the dark
changing faces a thousand times,
then slipping back into black water.

* * *

But they are confections, put-together things
who will not stay in or go out but pause
on the edge of a room or wherever they are,
uncertain of what they are or whether they care.
So are they praised for what they aren't, young,

and blamed for what they haven't, a wildness
of blood; pitiful creatures, calcined, watery,
with air-brushed bodies and brains.

* * *

I write this out of hard silence
to be rid of it. Not, as once, in love,
chin on breastbone as if the head
by its own dull weight would snap,
a green flower from a green stem.

LULLABY FOR A DAUGHTER

Go to sleep. Night is a coal pit
full of black water—
                night's a dark cloud
full of warm rain.

Go to sleep. Night is a flower
resting from bees—
                night's a green sea
swollen with fish.

Go to sleep. Night is a white moon
riding her mare—
                night's a bright sun
burned to black cinder.

Go to sleep,
night's come,
cat's day,
owl's day,
star's feast of praise,
moon to reign over
her sweet subject, dark.

SEQUENCE

1.

The mad have black roots in their brains
around which vessels clot and embrace
each other as mating snakes.

The roots feed on the brain until the brain
is all root—now the brain is gray
and suffocates in its own folds.

The brain grows smaller and beats
against its cage of bone
like a small wet bird.

Let us pity the mad we see every day,
the bird is dying without air and water
and growing smaller,
the air is cold, her beak is sharp,
the beating shriller.

2.

He loves her until
tomorrow or until 12:15 A.M.
when again he assumes the firedrake,
ricochets from the walls
in the exhaustion of kingship;
somewhere in his skull the Bible's leaves
seem turned by another's hand.

The pool table's green felt is earth,
ivory balls, people cracked toward leather holes.
Christ's blood is whiskey. Light is dark.
And light from a cave in whose furnace
three children continue their burning.

3.

The dead haloed in gladiolas
and electric organs,
those impossible hurts, trepanations,
the left eye punctured with glass;
he'll go to Canada with his dog,
a truly loved and loving creature—
fish in the water, bear in his den.
Not fox shrinking before foxhound
snaps its neck, horse cowered before crop.

4.

In the woods the low red bridge,
under it and above the flowing water,
spiders roost in girder's
rust and scale, flaking to touch.
Swift clear water. Soiled sand,
slippery green moss on rock face.
From the red bridge, years back
he dove into an eddy catching
the river's backward bend and swirl,
wishing not to swim on or in
as a duck and fish
but to be the water herself,
flowing then and still.

COLD AUGUST

The sun had shrunk to a dime,
passing behind the smallest
of clouds; the field was root
bare—shorthorns had grazed
it to leather. August's coldest
day when the green, unlike
its former self, returned to earth
as metal. Then from a swamp
I saw two large shadows floating
across the river, move up the sloping
bank, float swiftly as shadows against
the field toward where I stood.
I looked up as two great, red-tailed
hawks passed overhead; for an instant
I felt as prey then wheeled to watch
them disappear in southward course.
A day born in cold sourness
suffused me then in its dark,
brief image of magnificence.

NIGHT IN BOSTON

From the roof the night's the color
of a mollusk, stained with teeth and oil—
she wants to be rid of us and go to sea.

And the soot is the odor of brine
and imperishable sausages.

Beneath me from a window I hear "Blue Hawaii."
On Pontchartrain the Rex Club
dances on a houseboat in a storm—
a sot calms the water without wetting a foot.

I'd walk to Iceland, saluting trawlers.
I won't sell the rights to this miracle.

It was hot in Indiana.
The lovers sat on a porch swing, laughing;
a car passed on the gravel road,
red taillights bobbing over the ruts,
dust sweeping the house,
the scent of vetch from the pasture.

Out there the baleen nuzzles his iceberg,
monuments drown in the lava of birdshit.
I scuffle the cinders but the building doesn't shudder—
they've balanced it on a rock.
The Charles floats seaward, bored with history.

Night, cutting you open
I see you're full of sour air
like any rubber ball.

FEBRUARY SWANS

Of the hundred swans in West Bay
not one flies south in winter.
They breathe the dust of snow
swirling in flumes across the water,
white as their whiteness;
bones slighted by hunger
they move through the clots of ice,
heads looped low and tucked to the wind,
looking for fish in the deep greenness of water.

Now in the country, far from the Bay,
from a dark room I see a swan gliding
down the street, larger than a car, silent.
She'll need a fish the size of a human
to feed her hunger, so far from the water.
But there's nothing to eat between those snowbanks.
She looks toward my window. I think—
go back to the Bay, beautiful thing,
it was thirty below last night.
We gaze at each other until my breath
has glazed the window with frost.

NATURAL WORLD

1.

The earth is almost round. The seas
are curved and hug the earth, both
ends are crowned with ice.

The great Blue Whale swims near
this ice, his heart is warm
and weighs two thousand pounds,
his tongue weighs twice as much;
he weighs one hundred fifty tons.

There are so few of him left
he often can't find a mate;
he drags his six-foot sex
through icy waters,
flukes spread crashing.
His brain is large enough
for a man to sleep in.

2.

On Hawk Mountain in Pennsylvania
thousands upon thousands
upon thousands of hawks in migration
have been slaughtered for pleasure.
Drawn North or South in Spring and Fall:
Merlin and Kestrel, Peregrine, Gyrfalcon,
Marsh Hawk, Red-tailed, Sharp-tailed,
Sharp-shinned, Swainson's Hawk,
Golden Eagle and Osprey
slaughtered for pleasure.

MOVING

Not those who have lived here and gone
but what they have left: a worn-out broom,
coat hangers, the legs of a doll,
errors of possession to remind us of ourselves;
but for drunkenness or prayers the walls
collapse in boredom, or any new ecstasy
could hold them up, any moan or caress
or pillow-muffled laugh;
leaving behind as a gift seven rooms of air
once thought cathedral, those imagined
beasts at windows,
her griefs hung from the ceiling for spectacle.

But finally here I am often there
in its vacant shabbiness,
standing back to a window in the dark,
carried by the house as history, a boat,
deeper into a year, into the shadow
of all that happened there.

AFTER THE
ANONYMOUS SWEDISH

(17th century)

Deep in the forest there is a pond,
small, shaded by a pine so tall
its shadow crosses her surface.
The water is cold and dark and clear,
let it preserve those who lie at the bottom
invisible to us in perpetual dark.
It is our heaven, this bottomless
water that will keep us forever still;
though hands might barely touch they'll never
wander up an arm in caress or lift a drink;
we'll lie with the swords and bones
of our fathers on a bed of silt and pine needles.
In our night we'll wait
for those who walk the green and turning earth,
our brothers, even the birds and deer,
who always float down to us
with alarmed and startled eyes.

DAWN WHISKEY

Mind follow the nose
this honey of whiskey
I smell through the throat of the bottle.

I hear a wren in the maple
and ten million crickets,
leaf rustle
behind the wren and crickets,
farther back a faint dog bark.

And the glass is cool,
a sweet cedar post that flames so briskly.
Sight bear this honey
through the shell curved around the brain,
your small soft globes
pouring in new light—
remember things that burn with gold
as this whiskey to my tongue.

A YEAR'S CHANGES

This nadir: the wet hold
in which a beast heaps twigs and bits
of hair, bark and tree skin,
both food and turds mix in the warm
dust its body makes.
In winter the dream of summer,
in summer the dream of sleep,
in spring feasting,
living dreams through the morning.
Fall, my cancer, pared to bone,
I lost my fur, my bite gone dull,
all edges, red and showing; now naked,
February painted with ice, preserve me
in wakefulness—I wait for the rain,
to see a red pine free of snow,
my body uncrabbed, unleashed,
my brain alive.

* * *

In northern Manitoba
a man saw a great bald eagle—
hanging from its neck,
teeth locked in skin and feathers,
the bleached skull of a weasel.

* * *

To sing not instinct or tact,
wisdom,
the song's full stop and death,
but audible things, things moving
at noon in full raw light;
a dog moving around
the tree with the shade—
shade and dog in motion—
alive at noon in full natural light.

* * *

This nightflower, the size of a cat's head—
now moist and sentient—
let it hang there in the dark;
bare beauty asking nothing of us,
if we could graft you to us,
so singular and married to the instant.
But now rest picked, a trillium
never to repeat yourself. Soon enough
you'll know dead air, brief homage,
a sliver of glass in someone's brain.

* * *

Homesick for a dark, for clear black space
free of objects; to feel locked as wood
within a tree, a rock deep enough
in earth never to see the surface.

* * *

Snow. There's no earth left under it.
It's too cold to breathe.
Teeth ache, trees crack, the air is bluish.
My breath goes straight up.
This woods is so quiet
that if it weren't for the buffer of trees
I could hear everything on earth.

* * *

Only talk. Cloth after the pattern is cut,
discarded, spare wood barely kindling.
At night when the god in you trips,
hee-haws, barks and refuses to come
to tether. Stalk without quarry.
Yesterday I fired a rifle into the lake.

* * *

A cold spring dawn
near Parker Creek,
a doe bounding away through
shoulder-high fog
fairly floating,
soundless
as if she were running in a cloud.

* * *

That his death was disfigurement:
at impact when light passed
the cells yawned then froze in postures
unlike their former selves, teeth
stuck by the glue of their blood
to windshields, visors. And in the night,
a quiet snowy landscape, three bodies
slump, horribly rended.

* * *

Acacia Acidie Accipiter
flower boredom flight
gummy wet pale stemmed
barely above root level
and darkened by ferns;
but hawk
high now spots the cat he shot
and left there,
swings low
in narrowing circles,
feeds.

* * *

My mouth stuffed up with snow,
nothing in me moves,
Earth nudges all things this month.
I've outgrown this shell
I found in a sea of ice—

its drunken convolutions—
something should call me to another life.

* * *

Too cold for late May, snow flurries,
warblers tight in their trees, the air
with winter's clearness, dull
pearlish clear under clouds, clean
clear bite of wind, silver maple flexing
in the wind, wind rippling petals,
ripped from flowering crab,
pale pink against green firs, the body
chilled, blood unstirred, thick with frost:
body be snake,
self equal self to ground heat,
be wind cold, earth heated,
bend with tree, whip with grass,
move free clean and bright clear.

* * *

Night draws on him until he's soft
and blackened, he waits for bones
sharp-edged as broken stone, rubble
in a deserted quarry, to defoliate,
come clean and bare
come clean and dry,
for salt,
he waits for salt.

* * *

In the dark I think of the fire,
how hot the shed was when it burned,
the layers of tar paper and dry pine,
the fruitlike billows and blue embers,
the exhausted smell as of a creature
beginning to stink when it has no more to eat.

* * *

The doe shot in the back
and just below the shoulder
has her heart and lungs blown out.
In the last crazed seconds she leaves
a circle of blood on the snow.
An hour later we eat
her still-warm liver for lunch,
fried in butter with onions.
In the evening we roast
her loins, and drink two gallons of wine,
reeling drunken and yelling on the snow.
Jon Jackson will eat venison for a month,
he has no job, food or money,
and his pump and well are frozen.

* * *

June, sun high, nearly straight above,
all green things in short weak shadow;
clipping acres of pine for someone's
Christmas, forearms sore with trimming,
itching with heat—
drawing boughs away from a trunk
a branch confused with the thick
ugliness of a hognose snake.

* * *

Dogged days, dull, unflowering,
the mind petaled in cold wet dark;
outside the orange world is gray,
all things gray turned in upon
themselves in the globed eye of the seer—
gray seen.
But the orange world is orange to itself,
the war continues redly,
the moon is up in Asia,
the dark is only eight thousand miles deep.

* * *

At the edge of the swamp a thorn apple tree
beneath which partridge feed on red berries,
and an elm tipped over in a storm
opening a circle of earth formerly closed,
huge elm roots in a watery place, bare,
wet, as if there were some lid to let
secrets out or a place where the ground
herself begins, then grows outward
to surround the earth; the hole, a black
pool of quiet water, the white roots
of undergrowth. It appears bottomless,
an oracle I should worship at; I want
some part of me to be lost in it and return
again from its darkness, changing the creature,
or return to draw me back to a home.

LOCATIONS

*"I want this hardened arm to stop
dragging a cherished image."*—RIMBAUD

In the end you are tired of those places,
you're thirty, your only perfect three,
you'll never own another thing.
At night you caress them as if the tongue
turned inward could soothe, head lolling
in its nest of dark, the heart fibrotic,
inedible. Say that on some polar night
an eskimo thinks of his igloo roof, the blocks
of ice sculptured to keep out air, as the roof
of his skull; all that he is, has seen,
is pictured there—thigh with the texture
of the moon, whale's tooth burnished from use
as nothing, fixtures of place some delicate
as a young child's ear, close as snails to earth,
beneath the earth as earthworms, further beneath
as molten rock, into the hollow, vaulted place,
pure heat and pure whiteness,
where earth's center dwells.

You were in Harar but only for a moment,
rifles jostling blue barrels against blue barrels
in the ox cart, a round crater, hot, brown,
a bowl of hell covered with dust.

The angels you sensed in your youth
smelled strongly as a rattlesnake
smells of rotten cucumber, the bear
rising in the glade of ferns of hot fur
and sweat, dry ashes pissed upon.

You squandered your time as a mirror,
you kept airplanes from crashing at your doorstep,
they lifted themselves heavily to avoid your sign,
fizzling like matches in the Atlantic.

You look at Betelgeuse for the splendor
of her name but she inflames another universe.
Our smallest of suns barely touches earth
in the Gobi, Sahara, Mohavi, Matto Grosso.

Dumb salvages: there is a box made of wood,
cavernous, all good things are kept there,
and if the branches of ice that claw against the window
become hands, that is their business.

Yuma is an unbearable place.
The food has fire in it as
does the brazero's daughter
who serves the food in an orange dress
the color of a mussel's lip.
Outside it is hot as the crevasse
of her buttocks—perfect body temperature.
You have no idea where your body stops
and the heat begins.

On Lake Superior the undertow swallows
a child and no one notices until evening.
They often drown in the green water
of abandoned gravel pits,
or fall into earth where the crust is thin.

I have tried to stop the war.

You wanted to be a sculptor
creating a new shape that would exalt itself
as the shape of a ball or hand
or breast or dog or hoof,
paw print in snow, each cluster of grapes
vaguely different, bat's wing shaped
as half a leaf, a lake working
against its rim of ground.

You wear yellow this year for Christmas,
the color of Christ's wounds after three days,
the color of Nelse's jacket you wear when writing,
Nelse full of Guckenheimer, sloth, herring, tubercules.

There were sweet places to sleep: beds warmed
by women who get up to work or in the brush

beneath Coit Tower, on picnic tables in Fallon, Nevada
and Hastings, Nebraska, surrounded by giant curs,
then dew that falls like fine ice upon your face
in a bean field near Stockton, near a waterfall
in the Huron Mountains, memorable sleeps
in the bus stations of San Jose and Toledo, Ohio.

At the roller rink on Chippewa Lake
the skaters move to calliope music.
You watch a motorboat putt by the dock,
they are trolling for bass at night
and for a moment the boat and two men
are caught in the blue light of the rink,
then pass on slowly upon the black water.

Liquor has reduced you to thumbnails,
keratin, the scales of fish
your ancient relatives,
stranded in a rock pool.

O claritas, sweet suppleness
of breath,
love within a cloud that
blinds us
hear, speak, the world without.

Grove St., Gough St., Heber, Utah,
one in despair, two in disgust,
the third beneath the shadow
of a mountain wall, beyond
the roar of a diesel truck,
faintly the screech of lion.

Self immolation,
the heaviest of dreams—
you become a charcoal rick
for Christ, for man himself.
They laugh with you as you disappear
lying as a black log upon the cement,
the fire doused by your own blood.

The thunderstorm moved across the lake
in a sheet of rain, the lightning
struck a strawpile which burned in the night

with hot roars of energy
as in '48 when a jetplane crashed near town,
the pilot parachuting as a leaf through the red sky,
landing miles away, missing the fire.

There was one sun,
one cloud,
two horses running,
a leopard in chase;
only the one sun and a single cloud
a third across her face.
Above, the twelve moons of Jupiter
hissing in cold and darkness.

You worshipped the hindquarters
of beautiful women,
and the beautiful hindquarters of women
who were not beautiful;
the test was the hindquarters
as your father judged cattle.

He is standing behind a plow
in a yellow photograph,
a gangster hat to the back of his head,
in an undershirt with narrow straps,
reins over a shoulder waiting for the photo,
the horses with a foreleg raised,
waiting for the pull with impatience.

The cannon on the courthouse lawn was plugged,
useless against the japs.

In the dark barn
a stillborn calf on the straw,
rope to hoofs, its mother bawling
pulled nearly to death.

You've never been across the ocean,
you swept the auditorium with a broom
after the travel lectures and dreamed of going
but the maps have become old, the brain
set on the Mackenzie River, even Greenland
where dentists stalk polar bears from Cessnas.

The wrecked train smelled of camphor,
a bird floating softly above the steam,
the door of the refrigerator car cracked open
and food begins to perish in the summer night.

You've become sure that every year
the sky descends a little,
but there is joy in this pressure,
joy bumping against the lid
like a demented fly, a bird breaking
its neck against a picture window
while outside new gods roll over
in the snow in billowy sleep.

The oil workers sit on the curb
in front of the Blue Moon Bar & Cafe,
their necks red from the sun,
pale white beneath the collars
or above the sleeves; in the distance
you hear the clumping of the wells.
And at a friend's house
there are aunts and uncles, supper plates
of red beans and pork, a guitar is taken
from the wall—in the music
the urge of homesickness, a peach not to be held
or a woman so lovely but not to be touched,
some former shabby home far south of here,
in a warmer place.

Cold cement, a little snow upon it.
Where are the small gods who bless cells?
There are only men. Once you were in a room
with a girl of honey-colored hair,
the yellow sun streamed down air of yellow straw.
You owe it to yourself to despise this place,
the walls sift black powder,
you owe yourself a particular cave.
You wait for her, a stone in loamy stillness,
who will arrive with less pitiful secrets
from sidereal reaches, from other planets of the mind,
who beneath the chamber music of gown and incense
will reflect the damp sweetness of a cave.

[73]

At that farm there were so many hogs,
in the center of the pen in the chilled air
he straddles the pig and slits its throat,
blood gushes forth too dark to be blood,
gutted, singed, and scraped into pinkness
there are too many bowels, the organs
too large, pale sponges that are lungs,
the pink is too pink to understand.

This is earth I've fallen against,
there was no life before this;
                still icon
as if seen through mist,
cold liquid sun, blue falling
from the air,
                  foam of ship's prow
cutting water, a green shore beyond
the rocks;
beyond, a green continent.

from

OUTLYER

IN INTERIMS: OUTLYER

*"Let us open together the last
bud of the future."*—APOLLINAIRE

He Halts. He Haw. Plummets.
The snake in the river is belly up
diamond head caught in crotch of branch,
length wavering yellow with force of water.
Who strangles as this taste of present?
numen of walking and sleep, knees of snow
as the shark's backbone is gristle.
And if my sister hadn't died in an auto wreck
and had been taken by the injuns
I would have had something to do:
go into the mountains and get her back.

Miranda, I have proof that when people die
they become birds. And I've lost
my chance to go to sea or become a cowboy.
Age narrows me to this window and its
three week snow. This is Russia and I a clerk.
Miranda throws herself from the window
the ikon clutched to her breasts,
into the snow, over and over.

A world of ruminants, cloven-hoofed,
sum it: is it less worthless for being "in front"?
There are the others, ignorant of us
to a man: says Johnson of Lowell who
wouldn't come to tea who's he sunbitch
and he know armaments and cattle like
a Renaissance prince knew love & daggers
and faintly knew of Dante, or Cecco.
It is a world that belongs to Kipling.

What will I die with in my hand?
A paintbrush (for houses), an M15
a hammer or ax, a book a gavel
                a candlestick

tiptoeing upstairs.
What will I hold or will I
be caught with this usual thing
that I want to be my heart but
it is my brain and I turn it
over and over and over.

Only miracles should apply,
we have stones enough—
they steal all the heat and trip
everyone even the wary.
Throw stones away.

And
a tricky way of saying something unnecessary
will not do.

The girl standing outside the bus station
in Muskegon, Michigan hasn't noticed me.
I doubt she reads poetry or if she did
would like it at all or if she liked it
the affection would be casual and temporary.
She would anyway rather ride a horse
than read a poet, read a comic rather than
ride a poet. Sweetie, fifteen minutes
in that black alley bent over the garbage can
with me in the saddle would make
our affections equal. Let's be fair.

I love my dear daughter
her skin is so warm
and if I don't hurt her
she'll come to great harm.
I love my dog Missy
her skin is so warm,
I love all my friends
their skins are so warm,
my dear mother dead father
live sister dead sister
two brothers
their skins are so warm,
I love my lovely wife
her skin is most warm,

And I love my dear self
my skin is so warm,
I come to great harm.
I come to great harm.

I want to be told a children's story
that will stick.
I'm sorry I can't settle for less.
Some core of final delight.
In the funeral parlor my limbs
are so heavy I can't rise.
This isn't me in this nest of silk
but a relative bearing my face and name.
I still wanted to become a cowboy
or bring peace to the Middle East.
This isn't me. I saw Christ this summer
rising over the Absaroka Range.
Of course I was drunk.
I carry my vices to the wilderness.
That faintly blue person there among
the nasturtiums, among crooning relatives
and weeping wife, however, isn't me.

Where. We are born dead.
Our minds can taste this source
until that other death.
A long rain and we are children
and a long snow,
sleeping children in deep snow.

As in interims all journeys end
in three steps
with a mirrored door, beyond it a closet
and a closet wall.
And he wants to write poems to resurrect god,
to raise all buried things the eye
buries and the heart and brain, to
move wild laughter in the throat of death.

A new ax
a new ax
I'm going to play
with my new ax

sharp blue blade
handle of ash.
Then, exhausted, listen
to my new record, Johnny Cash.
Nine dollars in all,
two lovely things to play with
far better and more lasting
than a nine dollar whore
or two bottles of whiskey.
A new ax and Johnny Cash
sharp blue blade and handle of ash
O the *stream of your blood*
runs as black as the coal.

Saw ghosts not faintly or wispish,
loud they were raising on burly arms
at mid-day, witches' Sunday in full light,
murder in delight, all former dark things
in noonlight, all light things love
we perform at night and fuck as war wounds
rub, and sigh as others sighed, blind
in delight to the world outside the window.

When I began to make false analogies
between animals & humans, then countries,
Russia is like America and America like Russia,
the universe is the world and the world
a university, the teacher is a crayfish,
the poem is a bird and a housefly, a pig
without a poke, a flame and an oilcan,
a woman who never menstruates, a woman
without glands who makes love by generalized
friction; then I went to the country
to think of precision, O the moon
is the width of a woman's thigh.

The Mexican girl about fourteen years old
in the 1923 National Geographic found in the attic
when we thought the chimney was on fire and I stood
on the roof with snow falling looking down into
the black hole where the fire roared at the bottom.
The girl: lying in the Rio Grande in a thin

wet shift, water covering back between breasts
and buttocks but then isolate the buttocks
in the muddy water, two graceful melons from the deep
in the Rio Grande, to ride them up to the river's source
or down to the sea, it wouldn't matter, or I would
carry her like a pack into some fastness like
the Sawtooth Mountains. The melon butter of her
in water, myself in the cloudy brown water
as a fish beneath her.

All falseness flows: you would rust
in jerks, hobbles, they, dewlaps
sniff eglantine and in mint-cleared voices
not from dark but in puddles over cement,
an inch deep of watery mud: all falseness
flows; comes now, where should it rest?
Merlin, as Merlin, *le cri de Merlin,*
whose shores are never watched, as women
have no more than one mouth staring
at the ground; repeat now, from what cloud
or clouds or country, countries in dim sleep,
pure song, mouthless, as if a church buried
beneath the sea one bell tower standing
and one bell; staring for whom at ground's length,
elbows in ground, stare at me now: she grows
from the tree half vine and half woman
and haunts all my nights, as music can
that uses our tendons as chords, bowels to hurtle
her gifts; myths as Arcturus, Aldebaran
pictured as colored in with blood,
her eyes were bees and in her hair ice
seemed to glisten, drawn up as plants, the snake
wrapped around the crucifix knows, glass knows,
and O song, meal is made of us not even for small gods
who wait in the morning; dark pushes with no
to and fro, over and under, we who serve her
as canticles for who falls deeper, *breaks away,*
knows praise other than our own: sing.
Merely land and heavily drawn away from the sea
long before us, green has begun, every crevasse, kelp,
bird dung, froth of sea, foam over granite, wet

sea rose and roar of Baltic: who went from continent
to island, as wolves or elk would at night,
sea ice as salted glass, slight lid, mirror over
dark; as Odin least of all gods, with pine smell
of dark and animals crossed in winter
with whales butting shores,
dressed without heat in skins; said Christ who came
late, nothing to be found here, lovers of wood
not stone, north goes over and down, furthest from sun,
aloud in distance white wolf, whiter bear
with red mouth; they can eat flesh and nothing else.
        white winter
        white snow
        black trees
        green boughs
        over us
Arctic sun, one wildflower in profusion,
grass is blue, sterile fishless lake in rock
and northern lights shimmering, crackling.
As a child in mourning, mourned for, knows
how short and bittersweet, not less for saying again,
the child singing knows, near death, it is so alive,
brief and sweet, earth scarcely known, small
songs made of her, how large as hawk or tree,
only a stone lives beyond sweet things:
so that the sea raises herself not swallows
but pushed by wind and moon destroys them;
only dark gives light, Apollo, Christ,
only a blue and knotted earth broken by green
as high above gods see us in our sleeping end.
We know no other, curled as we are here,
sleep over earth, tongues, fog, thunder, wars.
Christ raises. Islands from the sea, see people come.
Clear your speech, it is all that we have,
aloud and here and now.

TRADER

I traded a girl
two apples for an orange.
I hate citrus
but she was beautiful.
As lovers we were rotten—
this was before the sexual revolution—
and we only necked and pawed,
"don't write below the lines!"
But now she's traded
that child's red mitten
I only touched
for a stovepipe hat,
four children,
and a milkman husband.
Soon I learn there will be no milkmen
and she'll want to trade again.
Stop. I won't take a giant Marianas
trench for two red apples.
You've had your orange
now lie in it.

HOSPITAL

Someone is screaming almost in Morse
code, three longs, a short, three
longs again. Man, woman, or animal?

Pale blue room. How many have died
here and will I with my ears drummed
to pain with three longs, one short, three longs?

It's never a yelp, it starts
far back in the throat
with three longs, a short, three longs.

All beasts everywhere listen to this.
It must be music to the gods—
three longs, one short, three longs.

I don't know who it is,
a beautiful woman with a lion's lungs
screaming three longs, one short, three longs?

COWGIRL

The boots were on the couch and had
manure on their heels and tips.

The cowgirl with vermilion udders and ears
that tasted of cream pulled on her jeans.

The saddle is not sore and the crotch with
its directionless brain is pounded by hammers.

Less like flowers than grease fittings women
win us to a life of holes, their negative space.

I don't know you and won't. You look at my hairline
while I work, conscious of history, in a bottomless lake.

Thighs that are indecently strong and have won the West,
I'll go back home where women are pliant as marshmallows.

DRINKING SONG

I want to die in the saddle. An enemy of civilization
I want to walk around in the woods, fish and drink.

I'm going to be a child about it and I can't help it, I was
born this way and it makes me very happy to fish and drink.

I left when it was still dark and walked on the path to the
river, the Yellow Dog, where I spent the day fishing and drinking.

After she left me and I quit my job and wept for a year and
all my poems were born dead, I decided I would only fish and drink.

Water will never leave earth and whiskey is good for the brain.
What else am I supposed to do in these last days but fish and drink?

In the river was a trout, and I was on the bank, my heart in my
chest, clouds above, she was in NY forever and I, fishing and drinking.

AWAKE

Limp with night fears: hellebore, wolfbane,
Marlowe is daggered, fire, volts, African vipers,
the grizzly the horses sensed, the rattlesnake
by the mailbox—how he struck at thrown rocks,
black water, framed by police, wanton wife,
I'm a bad poet broke and broken at thirty-two,
a renter, shot by mistake, airplanes and trains,
half-mast hardons, a poisoned earth, sun will
go out, car break down in a blizzard,
my animals die, fistfights, alcohol, caskets,
the hammerhead gliding under the boat near
Loggerhead Key, my soul, my heart, my brain,
my life so interminably struck with an ax
as wet wood splits bluntly, mauled into
sections for burning.

GHAZALS

I

Unbind my hair, she says. The night is white and warm,
the snow on the mountains absorbing the moon.

We have to get there before the music begins, scattered,
elliptical, needing to be drawn together and sung.

They have dark green voices and listening, there are birds,
coal shovels, the glazed hysteria of the soon-to-be-dead.

I suspect Jesus *will* return and the surprise will be
fatal. I'll ride the equator on a whale, a giraffe on land.

Even stone when inscribed bears the ecstatic. Pressed to
some new wall, ungiving, the screams become thinner.

Let us have the tambourine and guitars and forests, fruit,
and a new sun to guide us, a holy book, tracked in new blood.

II

I load my own shells and have a suitcase of pressed
cardboard. Naturally I'm poor and picturesque.

My father is dead and doesn't care if his vault leaks,
that his casket is cheap, his son a poet and a liar.

All the honest farmers in my family's past are watching
me through the barn slats, from the corncrib and hogpen.

Ghosts demand more than wives & teachers. I'll make a
"V" of my two books and plow a furrow in the garden.

And I want to judge the poetry table at the County Fair.
A new form, poems stacked in pyramids like prize potatoes.

This county agent of poetry will tell poets "more potash
& nitrogen, the rows are crooked and the field limp, depleted."

III

The alfalfa was sweet and damp in fields where shepherds
lay once and rams strutted and Indians left signs of war.

He harnessed the horses drawing the wagon of wheat toward
the road, ground froze, an inch of sifting snow around their feet.

She forks the hay into the mow, in winter is a hired girl
in town and is always tired when she gets up for school.

Asleep again between peach rows, drunk at midmorning and something
conclusive is needed, a tooth pulled, a fistfight, a girl.

Would any god come down from where and end a small war between
two walls of bone, brain veering, bucking in fatal velocity?

IV

Near a brown river with carp no doubt pressing their
round pursed mouths to the river's bed. Tails upward.

Watching him behind his heifer, standing on a milk
stool, flies buzzing and sister cows swishing tails.

In the tree house the separate nickels placed in her hand.
Skirt rises, her dog yelps below and can't climb ladders.

River and barn and tree. Field where wheat is scarcely high
enough to hide, in light rain knees on pebbles and March mud.

In the brain with Elinor and Sonia, Deirdre of course
in dull flare of peat and Magdalen fresh from the troops.

I want to be old, and old, young. With these few bodies at
my side in a creel with fresh ferns & flowers over them.

V

Yes yes yes it was the year of the tall ships
and the sea owned more and larger fish.

Antiquarians know that London's gutters were
pissed into openly and daggers worn by whores.

Smart's Geoffrey had distant relatives roaming
the docks hungry for garbage at dawn. Any garbage.

O Keats in Grasmere, walking, walking. Tom
is dead and this lover is loveless, loving.

Wordsworth stoops, laughs only once a month and then
in private, mourns a daughter on another shore.

But Keats' heart, Keats in Italy, Keats' heart
Keats how I love thee, I love thee John Keats.

VI

Now changed. None come to Carthage. No cauldrons, all love
comes without oily sacraments. Skin breathes cooler air.

And light was there and two cliff swallows hung and swooped
for flies, audible heat from the field where steers fed.

I'm going to Stonehenge to recant, or from the manure pile
behind this shed I'm going to admit to a cow I've lied.

He writes with a putty knife and goo, at night the North Star
hangs on the mountain peak like a Christmas ornament.

On the table the frozen rattlesnake thaws, the perfect club!
the perfect crime! soon now to be skinned for my hatband.

VII

Says he ah Edward I too have a dark past of manual labor.
But now Trivium Charontis seem to want me for Mars.

If her thighs weigh 21 pounds apiece what do her lips weigh?
Do that trick where you touch your toes. Do that right now.

The bold U.S.A. cowpoke in Bozeman, Montana, hates hippies,
cuts off their hair, makes $200 a month, room and board.

We want the sow bear that killed Clark's sheep to go away.
She has two cubs but must die for her terrible appetite.

Girl-of-my-dreams if you'll be mine I'll give up poetry
and be your index finger, lapdog, donkey, obvious unicorn.

VIII

The color of a poppy and bruised, the subalpine green that
ascends the mountainside from where the eagle looked at sheep.

Her sappy brain fleers, is part of the satin shirt (western) she
wears, chartreuse with red scarf. Poeet he says with two *e*'s!

The bull we frighten by waving our hats bellows, his pecker
lengthens touching the grass, he wheels, foam from the mouth.

How do we shoot those things that don't even know they're animals
grazing and stalking in the high meadow: puma elk grizzly deer.

When he pulled the trigger the deer bucked like a horse, spine
broken, grew pink in circles, became a lover kissing him goodnight.

IX

He said the grizzly sat eating the sheep and when the bullet
struck tore the sheep in two, fell over backward dead.

With her mouth warm or cold she remains a welcome mat, a hole
shot through it many years ago in Ohio. Hump. Hemp treaded.

Is there an acre left to be allotted to each man & beast so
they might regard each other on hands and knees behind fences?

The sun straight above was white and aluminum and the trout
on the river bottom watched his feet slip clumsily on the rocks.

I want an obscene epitaph, one that will disgust the Memorial
Day crowds so that they'll indignantly topple my gravestone.

X

Praise me at Durkheim Fair where I've never been, hurling
grenade wursts at those who killed my uncle back in 1944.

Nothing is forgiven. The hurt child is thirty-one years old
and the girl in the pale blue dress walks out with another.

Where love lies. In the crawl space under the back porch
thinking of the aunt seen shedding her black bathing suit.

That girl was rended by the rapist. I'll send her a healing
sonnet in heaven. Forgive us. Forgive us. Forgive us.

The moon I saw through her legs beneath the cherry tree had
no footprints on it and a thigh easily blocked out its light.

Lauren Hutton has replaced Norma Jean, Ava Gardner, Lee Remick
and Vanessa Redgrave in my Calvinist fantasies. Don't go away.

XI

The brain opens the hand which touches that spot, clinically
soft, a member raises from his chair and insists upon his rights.

In some eyebank a cornea is frozen in liquid nitrogen. One day
my love I'll see your body from the left side of my face.

Half the team, a Belgian mare, was huge though weak. She died
convulsively from the 80-volt prod, still harnessed to her mate.

Alvin C. shot the last wolf in the Judith Basin after a four-year
hunt, raising a new breed of hounds to help. Dressed out 90 lbs.

When it rains I want to go north into the taiga, and before I
freeze in arid cold watch the reindeer watch the northern lights.

XII

Says Borges in *Ficciones* "I'm in hell. I'm dead," and the dark
is glandular and swells about my feet concealing the ground.

Let us love the sun, little children but it is around too
much to notice and has no visible phases to care about.

Two pounds of steak eaten in deference to a tequila hang-over.
His sign is that of a pig, a thousand-pound Hampshire boar.

Some would say her face looked homely with that thing sticking
out of it as if to feed her. Not I, said Wynken, not I.

The child is fully clothed but sits in the puddle madly
slapping the warm water on which the sun ripples and churns.

XIII

The night is thin and watery; fish in the air
and moon glint off her necklace of human teeth.

Bring O bring back my Bonnie and I'll return yours
with interest and exhaustion. I'm stuck between those legs.

Dangers of drugs: out in the swamp's middle he's stoned
and a bear hound mammothly threatens. Dazed with fright.

Marcia I won't go to Paris—too free with your body—
it's mine it's mine it's mine not just everyone's.

Now in this natal month Christ must be in some distant
nebula. O come down right now and be with us.

In the hole he fell in, a well pit, yellow jackets stung
him to death. Within minutes death can come by bees.

XIV

That heartless finch, botulic. An official wheeze passes through
the screen door into the night, the vision of her finally dead.

I've decided here in Chico, Montana, that Nixon isn't president
and that that nasty item, Agnew, is retired to a hamster farm.

And that those mountains hold no people but geologists
spying on each other, and beasts spying on the geologists.

Mule deer die from curiosity—what can that thing be
wandering around with a stick, forgotten from last year?

Some tourists confuse me for an actual cowboy, ecstasy in
deceit, no longer a poet but a bonafide paper buckaroo.

I offer a 21-gun salute to the caress as the blackflies buzz
around me and the rotting elk hides. The true source of the stink.

XV

Why did this sheep die? The legs are thin, stomach hugely
bloated. The girl cries and kicks her legs on the sofa.

The new marvels of language don't come up from the depths
but from the transparent layer, the soiled skin of things.

In London for puissant literary reasons he sits with the other
lost ones at a Soho striptease show. An endless oyster bar.

We'll need miracles of art and reason to raise these years
which are tombstones carved out of soap by the world's senators.

We'll have to move out at dawn and the dew is only a military
metaphor for the generally felt hidden-behind-bushes sorrow.

XVI

It is an hour before dawn and even prophets sleep
on their beds of gravel. Dreams of fish & hemlines.

The scissors moves across the paper and through
the beard. It doesn't know enough or when to stop.

The bear tires of his bicycle but he's strapped on
with straps of silver and gold straps inlaid with scalps.

We are imperturbable as deer whose ancestors saw the last
man and passed on the sweet knowledge by shitting on graves.

Let us arrange to meet sometime in transit, we'll all take
the same train perhaps, Cendrars' Express or the defunct Wabash.

Her swoon was officially interminable with unconvincing
geometric convulsions, no doubt her civic theater experience.

XVII

O Atlanta, roseate dawn, the clodhoppers, hillbillies, rednecks,
drunken dreams of murdering blacks; the gin mills still.

Our fried chicken and Key lime pie and rickets. To drain all
your swamps and touch a match, Seminoles forbidden drink.

Save the dogs everywhere. In France by actual count, Count
Blah Blah shot 885 pheasants in one day, his personal record.

There was a story of a lost child who remained lost & starved
to death hiding in a hollow log from both animals and searchers.

Cuba is off there beyond the Tortugas, forever invisible; Isle
of Pines where Crane wept, collecting tons of starfish and eels.

Her love was committed to horses and poets weighing less than
150 lbs. I weigh 200 and was not allowed into her Blue Fuck Room.

XVIII

I told the dark-haired girl to come down out of the apple
tree and take her medicine. In a dream I told her so.

We're going to have to do something about the night. The tissue
won't restore itself in the dark. I feel safe only at noon.

Waking. Out by the shed, their home, the chicano cherrypickers
sing hymns on a hot morning, three guitars and a concertina.

We don't need dimestore surrealists buying objects to write
about or all this up-against-the-wall nonsense in *Art News.*

Even in the wilderness, in Hell Roaring Creek Basin, in this
grizzly kingdom, I fear stepping into a hidden missile silo.

My friend has become crippled, back wrenched into an "S" like
my brain. We'll go to Judah to wait for the Apocalypse.

XIX

We were much saddened by Bill Knott's death.
When he reemerged as a hospital orderly we were encouraged.

Sad thoughts of different cuts of meat and how I own no
cattle and am not a rancher with a freezer full of prime beef.

A pure plump dove sits on the wire as if two wings emerged
from a russet pear, head tucked into the sleeping fruit.

Your new romance is full of nails hidden from the saw's teeth,
a board under which a coral snake waits for a child's hand.

I don't want to die in a foreign land and was only in one
once, England, where I felt near death in the Cotswolds.

The cattle walked in the shallow water and birds flew
behind them to feed on the disturbed insects.

XX

Some sort of rag of pure language, no dictums but a bell
sound over clear water, beginning day no. 245 of a good year.

The faces made out of leaves and hidden within them, faces
that don't want to be discovered or given names by anyone.

There was a virgin out walking the night during the plague when
the wolves entered Avila for carrion. The first took her neck.

The ninth month when everything is expected of me and nothing
can be told—September when I sit and watch the summer die.

She knelt while I looked out the car window at a mountain
(Emigrant Peak). We need girls and mountains frequently.

If I can clean up my brain, perhaps a stick of dynamite will
be needed, the Sibyl will return as an undiscovered lover.

XXI

He sings from the bottom of a well but she can hear him up
through the oat straw, toads, boards, three entwined snakes.

It quiets the cattle they say mythically as who alive has
tried it, their blank stares, cows digesting song. Rumen.

Her long hissing glides at the roller-skating rink, skates
to calves to thighs to ass in blue satin and organ music.

How could you be sane if 250,000 came to the Isle of Wight
to hear your songs near the sea and they looked like an ocean.

Darling companion. We'll listen until it threatens and walls
fall to trumpet sounds or not and this true drug lifts us up.

That noise that came to us out in the dark, grizzly, leviathan,
drags the dead horse away to hollow swelling growls.

XXII

Maps. Maps. Maps. Venezuela, Keewanaw, Iceland open up
unfolding and when I get to them they'll look like maps.

New pilgrims everywhere won't visit tombs, need living
monuments to live again. But there are only tombs to visit.

They left her in the rain tied to the water with cobwebs,
stars stuck like burrs to her hair. I found her by her wailing.

It's obvious I'll never go to Petersburg and Akhmadulina
has married another in scorn of my worship of her picture.

You're not fooling yourself—if you weren't a coward you'd be
another target in Chicago, tremulous bulls-eye for hog fever.

XXIII

I imagined her dead, killed by some local maniac who
crept upon the house with snowmobile at low throttle.

Alcohol that lets me play out hates and loves and fights;
in each bottle is a woman, the betrayer and the slain.

I insist on a one-to-one relationship with nature.
If Thursday I'm a frog it will have to be my business.

You are well. You grow taller. Friends think I've bought you
stilts but it is I shrinking, up past my knees in marl.

She said take out the garbage. I trot through a field with the
sack in my teeth. At the dump I pause to snarl at a rat.

XXIV

This amber light floating strangely upward in the woods—nearly
dark now with a warlock hooting through the tips of trees.

If I were to be murdered here as an Enemy of the State you would
have to bury me under that woodpile for want of a shovel.

She was near the window and beyond her breasts I could see
the burdock, nettles, goldenrod in a field beyond the orchard.

We'll have to abandon this place and live out of the car again.
You'll nurse the baby while we're stuck in the snow out of gas.

The ice had entered the wood. It was twenty below and the beech
easy to split. I lived in a lean-to covered with deerskins.

I have been emptied of poison and returned home dried
out with a dirty bill of health and screaming for new wine.

XXV

O happy day! said *overpowered*, had by it all and transfixed
and unforgetting other times that refused to swirl and flow.

The calendar above my head made of unnatural numbers, day
lasted five days and I expect a splendid year's worth of dawn.

Rain pumps. Juliet in her tower and Gaspara Stamp again and
that girl lolling in the hammock with a fruit smell about her.

Under tag alder, beneath the ferns, crawling to know animals
for hours, how it looks to them down in this lightless place.

The girl out in the snows in the Laurentians saves her money
for Montreal and I am to meet her in a few years by "accident."

Magdalen comes in a waking dream and refuses to cover me,
crying out for ice, release from time, for a cool spring.

XXVI

What will I do with seven billion cubic feet of clouds
in my head? I want to be wise and dispense it for quarters.

All these push-ups are making me a muscular fatman. Love would
make me lean and burning. Love. Sorry the elevator's full.

She was zeroed in on by creeps and forgot my meaningful glances
from the door. But then I'm walleyed and wear used capes.

She was built entirely of makeup, greasepaint all the way through
like a billiard ball is a billiard ball beneath its hard skin.

We'll have to leave this place in favor of where the sun
is cold when seen at all, bones rust, it rains all day.

The cat is mine and so is the dog. You take the orchard,
house and car and parents. I'm going to Greenland at dawn.

XXVII

I want a sign, a heraldic bird, or even an angel at midnight
or a plane ticket to Alexandria, a room full of good dreams.

This won't do; farmlife with chickens clucking in the barnyard,
lambs, cows, vicious horses kicking when I bite their necks.

The woman carved of ice was commissioned by certain unknown
parties and lasted into a March thaw, tits turning to water.

Phone call. That strange cowboy who pinned a button to the boy's
fly near the jukebox—well last night he shot his mom.

Arrested, taken in as it were for having a purple fundament,
a brain full of grotesqueries, a mouth exploding with red lies.

Hops a plane to NYC riding on the wing through a thunderstorm,
a parade, a suite at the Plaza, a new silver-plated revolver.

XXVIII

In the hotel room (far above the city) I said I bet you
can't crawl around the room like a dog hoho. But she could!

All our cities are lewd and slippery, most of all San Francisco
where people fuck in the fog wearing coarse wool.

And in Los Angeles the dry heat makes women burn so that
lubricants are fired in large doses from machine guns.

We'll settle the city question by walking deeply into forests
and in reasonably vestal groves eat animal meat and love.

I'm afraid nothing can be helped and all letters must be
returned unopened. Poetry must die so poems will live again.

Mines: there were no cities of golden-haired women down there
but rats, raccoon bones, snake skeletons and dark. Black dark.

XXIX

For my horse Brotherinlaw who had no character
breaking into panic at first grizzly scent.

Stuff this up your ass New York City you hissing
clip joint and plaster-mouthed child killer.

In Washington they eat bean soup and there's
bean soup on the streets and in the mouths of monuments.

The bull in the grove of lodgepole pines, a champion
broke his prick against a cow and is now worthless.

For that woman whose mouth has paper burns
a fresh trout, salt, honey, and healing music.

XXX

I am walked on a leash by my dog and am water
only to be crossed by a bridge. Dog and bridge.

An ear not owned by a face, an egg without a yolk
and my mother without a rooster. Not to have been.

London has no bees and it is bee time. No hounds
in the orchard, no small craft warnings or sailing ships.

In how many poems through how many innocent branches
has the moon peeked without being round.

This song is for New York City who peeled me like
an apple, the fat off the lamb, raw and coreless.

XXXI

I couldn't walk across that bridge in Hannibal
at night. I was carried in a Nash Ambassador.

On Gough Street the cars went overhead. I counted
two thousand or more one night before I slept.

She hit him in the face with her high-heel shoe
as he scrambled around the floor getting away.

What am I going to do about the mist and the canning
factory in San Jose where I loaded green beans all night?

Billions of green beans in the Hanging Gardens off Green
Street falling softly on our heads, the dread dope again.

XXXII

All those girls dead in the war from misplaced or aimed
bombs, or victims of the conquerors, some eventually happy.

My friends he said after midnight you all live badly.
Dog's teeth grew longer and wife in bed became a lizard.

Goddamn the dark and its shrill violet hysteria.
I want to be finally sane and bow to all sentient creatures.

I'll name all the things I know new and old and you may
select from the list and remember the list but forget me.

It was cold and windy and the moon blew white fish across
the surface where phosphorescent tarpon swam below.

Ice in the air and the man just around the corner has a gun
and that nurse threw a tumor at you from the hospital window.

XXXIII

That her left foot is smaller if only slightly
than her right and when bare cloven down to the arch.

Lovers when they are up and down and think they are whirling
look like a pink tractor tire from the ceiling.

Drag the wooden girl to the fire but don't throw
her in as would the Great Diana of Asia.

Oh the price, the price price. Oh the toll, the toll toll.
Oh the cost, the cost cost. Of her he thought.

To dogs and fire, Bengal tiger, gorilla, Miura bull
throw those who hate thee, let my love be perfect.

I will lift her up out of Montana where her hoof
bruised my thigh. I planted apple trees all day.

XXXIV

When she walked on her hands and knees in the Arab
chamber the flyrod, flies, the river became extinct.

When I fall out of the sky upon you again I'll
feather at the last moment and come in feet first.

There are rotted apples in the clover beneath the fog
and mice invisibly beneath the apples eat them.

There is not enough music. The modal chord I carried
around for weeks is lost for want of an instrument.

In the eye of the turtle and the goldfish and the dog
I see myself upside down clawing the floor.

XXXV

When she dried herself on the dock a drop of water
followed gravity to her secret place with its time lock.

I've been sacrificed to, given up for, had flowers
left on my pillow by unknown hands. The last is a lie.

How could she cheat on me with that African? Let's refer
back to the lore of the locker room & shabby albino secrets.

O the shame of another's wife especially a friend's.
Even a peek is criminal. That greener grass is brown.

Your love for me lasted no longer than my savings for Yurup.
I couldn't bear all those photos of McQueen on your dresser.

Love strikes me any time. The druggist's daughter, the 4-H
girl riding her blue-ribbon horse at canter at the fair.

XXXVI

A scenario: I'm the Star, Lauren, Faye, Ali, little stars,
we tour America in a '59 Dodge, they read my smoldering poems.

I climbed the chute and lowered myself onto the Brahma bull,
we jump the fence trampling crowds, ford rivers, are happy.

All fantasies of a life of love and laughter where I hold your
hand and watch suffering take the very first boat out of port.

The child lost his only quarter at the fair but under the grandstand
he finds a tunnel where all cowshit goes when it dies.

His epitaph: he could dive to the bottom or he paddled in black
water or bruised by flotsam he drowned in his own watery sign.

In the morning the sky was red as were his eyes and his brain
and he rolled over in the grass soaked with dew and said no.

XXXVII

Who could knock at this door left open, repeat
this after me and fold it over as an endless sheet.

I love or I am a pig which perhaps I should be,
a poisoned ham in the dining room of Congress.

Not to kill but to infect with mercy. You are known
finally by what magazines you read in whose toilet.

I'll never be a cocksman or even a butterfly. The one
because I am the other, and the other, the other one.

This is the one song sung loud though in code: I love.
A lunepig shot with fatal poison, butterfly, no one.

XXXVIII

Once and for all to hear, I'm not going to shoot anybody
for any revolution. I'm told it hurts terribly to be shot.

Think that there are miniature pools of whiskey in your flesh
and small deposits of drugs and nicotine encysted in fat.

Beautiful enchanted women (or girls). Would you take your
places by my side, or do you want to fuck up your lives elsewhere?

The veteran said it was "wall-to-wall death" as the men had
been eating lunch, the mortar had hit, the shack blown to pieces.

We'll pick the first violets and mushrooms together & loiter
idyllically in the woods. I'll grow goat feet & prance around.

Master, master, he says, where can I find a house & living
for my family, without blowing my whole life on nonsense?

XXXIX

If you laid out all the limbs from the Civil War hospital
in Washington they would encircle the White House seven times.

Alaska cost two cents per acre net and when Seward
slept lightly he talked to his wife about ice.

My heart is Grant's for his bottle a day and his
foul mouth, his wife that weighed over five hundred pounds.

A hundred years later Walt Whitman often still
walks the length of the Potomac and *on* the water.

A child now sees it as a place for funerals and bags
of components beneath the senators' heads.

XL

If you were less of a vowel or had a full stop in your
brain. A cat's toy, a mouse stuffed with cotton.

It seems we must reject the ovoid for the sphere,
the sphere for the box, the box for the eye of the needle.

And the world for the senate for the circus
for the war for a fair for a carnival. The hobbyhorse.

The attic for a drawer and the drawer for a shell.
The shell for the final arena of water.

That fish with teeth longer than its body is ours
and the giant squid who scars the whale with sucker marks.

XLI

Song for Nat King Cole and the dog who ate the baby
from the carriage as if the carriage were a bowl.

A leafy peace & wormless earth we want, no wires,
connections, struts or props, only guitars and flutes.

The song of a man with a dirty-minded wife—there is
smoke from her pit which is the pit of a peach.

I wrenched my back horribly chopping down a tree—quiff,
quim, queeritus, peter hoister, pray for torn backs.

The crickets are chirping tonight and an ant crosses
the sleeping body of a snake to get to the other side.

I love the inventions of men, the pea sheller, the cherry
picker, the hay baler, the gun and throne and grenade.

XLII

New music might, that sucks men down in howls
at sea, please us if trapped in the inner ear.

When rising I knew there was a cock in that dream
where it shouldn't have been I confess I confess.

Say there this elbow tips glass upward, heat rolls
down in burns, say hallow this life hid under liquid.

Late in the morning Jesus ate his second breakfast,
walked out at five years, drove his first nail into a tree.

Say the monkey's jaw torn open by howling, say after
the drowned man's discovered scowling under the harbor's ice.

XLIII

Ghazal in fear there might not be another
to talk into fine white ash after another blooms.

He dies from it over and over; Duncan has
his own earth to walk through. Let us borrow it.

Mary is Spanish and from her heart comes forth
a pietà of withered leather, all bawling bulls.

Stand in the wine of it, the clear cool gold
of this morning and let your lips open now.

The fish on the beach that the blackbirds eat
smell from here as dead men might after war.

XLIV

That's a dark trough we'd hide in. Said his
sleep without *frisson* in a meadow beyond Jupiter.

It is no baronet of earth to stretch to—flags
planted will be only flags where no wind is.

Hang me rather there or the prez' jowel on a stick
when we piss on the moon as a wolf does NNW of Kobuk.

I'll be south on the Bitteroot while you're up there
and when you land I'll fire a solitary shot at moonface.

I wish you ill's ills, a heavy thumb & slow hands
and may you strike hard enough to see nothing at all.

XLV

What in coils works with riddle's logic, Riemann's
time a cluster of grapes moved and moving, convolute?

As nothing is separate from Empire the signs change
and move, now drawn outward, not "about" but "in."

The stars were only stars. If I looked up then it was
to see my nose flaring on another's face.

Ouspensky says, from one corner the mind looking for
herself may go to another then another as I went.

And in literal void, dazzling dark, who takes
who where? We are happened upon and are found a home.

XLVI

O she buzzed in my ear "I love you" and I dug at
the tickle with a forefinger with which I *knew* her.

At the post office I was given the official FBI
Eldridge Cleaver poster—"guess he ain't around here."

The escaping turkey vulture vomits his load of rotten
fawn for quick flight. The lesson is obvious & literary.

We are not going to rise again. Simple as that.
We are not going to rise again. Simple as that.

I say it from marrow depth I miss my tomcat gone now from
us three months. He was a fellow creature and I loved him.

XLVII

The clouds swirling low past the house and
beneath the tree tops and upstairs windows, tin thunder.

On the hill you can see far out at sea a black ship
burying seven hundred yards of public grief.

The fish that swam this morning in the river swims
through the rain in the orchard over the tips of grass.

Spec. Forces Sgt. Clyde Smith says those fucking
VC won't come out in the open and fight. O.K. Corral.

This brain has an abscess which drinks whiskey
turning the blood white and milky and thin.

The white dog with three legs dug a deep
hole near the pear tree and hid herself.

XLVIII

Dog, the lightning frightened us, dark house and both of us
silvered by it. Now we'll have three months of wind and cold.

Safe. From miracles and clouds, cut off from you and your
earthly city, parades of rats, froth, and skull tympanums.

The breathing in the thicket behind the beech tree was a deer
that hadn't heard me, a doe. I had hoped for a pretty girl.

Flickers gathering, swallows already gone. I'm going south
to the Yucatan or Costa Rica and foment foment and fish.

In the sudan grass waving, roots white cords, utterly hidden
and only the hounds could find me assuming someone would look.

The sun shines coldly. I aim my shotgun at a ship at sea
and say nothing. The dog barks at the ship and countless waves.

XLIX

After the "invitation" by the preacher she collapsed in the
aisle and swallowed her tongue. It came back out when pried.

No fire falls and the world is wet not to speak of gray and
heat resistant. This winter the snow will stay forever.

The dead cherry trees diseased with leaf rot were piled and
soaked with fuel oil, flames shooting upward into the rain.

Rouse your soul to frenzy said Pasternak. Icons built
of flesh with enough heat to save a life from water.

A new sign won't be given and the old ones you forgot won't
return again until the moment before you die, unneeded then.

Fuse is wet, match won't light it and nothing will. Heat comes
out of the center, radiates faintly and no paper will burn.

L

A boot called Botte Sauvage renders rattlers harmless but they
cost too much; the poet bitten to death for want of boots.

I'm told that black corduroy offers protection from moonburn
and that if you rub yourself with a skunk women will stay away.

There is a hiding place among the relics of the Fifties, poets
hiding in the trunks of Hudson Hornets off the Merritt Parkway.

They said she was in Rome with her husband, a sculptor, but
I'm not fooled. At the Excelsior I'll expose her as a whore.

Down in the canyon the survivors were wailing in the overturned
car but it was dark, the cliffs steep so we drove on to the bar.

She wants affection but is dressed in aluminum siding and her
edges are jagged; when cold, the skin peels off the tongue at touch.

LI

Who could put anything together that would stay in one place
as remorseless as that cabin hidden in the maple grove.

In Nevada the whores are less clean and fresh than in
Montana, and do not grow more beautiful with use.

The car went only seventeen miles before the motor burned up
and I sat in the grass thinking I had been taken and was sad.

This toothache means my body is wearing out, new monkey glands
for ears in the future, dog teeth, a pink transplanted body.

She is growing old. Of course with the peach, apple, plum,
you can eat around the bruised parts but still the core is black.

Windemere and Derwent Water are exhausted with their own
charm and want everyone to go back to their snot-nosed slums.

LII

I was lucky enough to have invented a liquid heart
by drinking a full gallon of DNA stolen from a lab.

To discover eleven more dollars than you thought you
had and the wild freedom in the tavern that follows.

He's writing mood music for the dead again and ought to have
his ass kicked though it is bruised too much already by his sport.

Both serpent becoming dragon and the twelve moons lost
at sea, worshipped items, rifts no longer needed by us.

Hot mickey mouse jazz and the mice jigging up the path
to the beehive castle, all with the bleached faces of congressmen.

LIII

These corners that stick out and catch on things
and I don't fill my body's clothes.

Euclid, walking in switchbacks, kite's tip, always
either *up* or *down* or both, triangular tongue & cunt.

Backing up to the rose tree to perceive which of its
points touch where. I'll soon be rid of you.

There are no small people who hitch rides on snakes
or ancient people with signs. I am here now.

That I will be suicided by myself or that lids close over
and over simply because they once were open.

We'll ask you to leave this room and brick up the door
and all the doors in the hallway until you go outside.

LIV

Aieeee was said in a blip the size of an ostrich egg,
blood pressures to a faint, humming heart flutters.

I can't die in this theater—the movie, *Point Blank,*
god's cheap abuse of irony. But the picture is fading.

This dry and yellow heat where each chicken's
scratch uproots a cloud and hay bursts into flame.

The horse is enraged with flies and rolls over
in the red dirt until he is a giant liver.

From the mailman's undulant car and through the lilacs
the baseball game. The kitchen window is white with noon.

LV

The child crawls in widening circles, backs to the wall
as a dog would. The lights grow dim, his mother talks.

Swag: a hot night and the clouds running low were brains and I
above them with the moon saw down through a glass skull.

And O god I think I want to sleep within some tree
or on a warmer planet beneath a march of asteroids.

He saw the lady in the Empire dress raise it to sit bare
along the black tree branch where she sang a ditty of nature.

They are packing up in the lamplight, moving out again
for the West this time sure only of inevitable miracles.

No mail delights me as much as this—written with plum juice
on red paper and announcing the rebirth of three dead species.

LVI

God I am cold and want to go to sleep for a long time
and only wake up when the sun shines and dogs laugh.

I passed away in my sleep from general grief and a seven
year hangover. Fat angels wrapped me in traditional mauve.

A local indian maiden of sixteen told the judge to go
fuck himself, got thirty days, died of appendicitis in jail.

I molded all the hashish to look like deer & rabbit turds
and spread them in the woods for rest stops when I walk.

Please consider the case closed. Otis Redding died in a
firestorm and we want to put him together again somehow.

LVII

I thought it was night but found out the windows were painted
black and a bluebird bigger than a child's head was singing.

When we get out of NAM the pilot said we'll go down to S.A.
and kick the shit outa those commie greasers. Of course.

In sleep walking all year long I grew cataracts, white-haired,
flesh fattened, texture of mushrooms, whistled notes at moon.

After seven hours of television and a quart of vodka he wept
over the National Anthem. O America Carcinoma the eagle dead.

Celebrate her with psalms and new songs—she'll be fifteen
tomorrow, a classic beauty who won't trouble her mind with poems.

I wanted to drag a few words out of silence then sleep and none
were what I truly wanted. So much silence and so many words.

LVIII

These losses are final—you walked out of the grape arbor
and are never to be seen again and you aren't aware of it.

I set off after the grail seven years ago but like a spiral
from above these circles narrow, tighten into a single point.

Let's forgive her for her chinese-checker brain and the pills
that charge it electrically. She's pulled the switch too often.

After the country dance in the yellow Buick Dynaflow with
leather seats we thought Ferlin Husky was singing to us.

A bottle of Corbys won you. A decade later on hearing
I was a poet you laughed. You are permanently coarsened.

Catherine near the lake is a tale I'm telling—a whiff
of lilac and a girl bleeds through her eyes like a pigeon.

LIX

On the fourteenth Sunday after Pentecost I rose early
and went fishing where I saw an osprey eat a bass in a tree.

We are not all guilty for anything. Let all stupefied
Calvinists take pleasure in sweet dirty pictures and gin.

As an active farmer I'm concerned. Apollinaire fertilizer
won't feed the pigs or chickens. Year of my seventh failure.

When we awoke the music was faint and a golden light came
through the window, one fly buzzed she whispered another's name.

Let me announce I'm not against homosexuality. Now that the air
is clear on this issue you can talk freely Donny Darkeyes.

A home with a heated garage where dad can tinker with his
poetry on a workbench and mom glazes the steamed froth for lunch.

LX

She called from Sundance, Wyoming, and said the posse had
forced her into obscene acts in the motel. Bob was dead.

The horse kicked the man off his feet and the man rolled
screaming in the dirt. The red-haired girl watched it all.

I've proclaimed June Carter queen-of-song as she makes me
tremble, tears form, chills come. I go to the tavern and drink.

The father ran away and was found near a highway underpass
near Fallon, Nevada, where he looked for shelter from the rain.

My friend the poet is out there in the West being terrified,
he wants to come home and eat well in New York City.

Daddy is dead and late one night won't appear on the porch
in his hunting clothes as I've long wanted him to. He's dead.

[119]

LXI

Wondering what this new light is, before he died he walked
across the kitchen and said "My stomach is very cold."

And this haze, yellowish, covers all this morning, meadow,
orchard, woods. Something bad is happening somewhere to her.

I was ashamed of her Appalachian vulgarity and vaguely askew
teeth, her bad grammar, her wanting to screw more often than I.

It was May wine and the night liquid with dark and fog when
we stopped the car and loved to the sound of frogs in the swamp.

I'm bringing to a stop all my befouled nostalgia about childhood.
My eye was gored out, there was a war and my nickname was pig.

There was an old house that smelled of kerosene and apples
and we hugged in a dark attic, not knowing how to continue.

LXII

He climbed the ladder looking over the wall at the party
given for poets by the Prince of China. Fun was had by all.

A certain gracelessness entered his walk and gestures. A tumor
the size of a chick-pea grew into a pink balloon in his brain.

I won't die in Paris or Jerusalem as planned but by electrocution
when I climb up the windmill to unscrew the shorted yard lights.

Samadhi. When I slept in the woods I awoke before dawn
and drank brandy and listened to birds until the moon disappeared.

When she married she turned from a beautiful girl into a
useless sow with mud on her breasts and choruses of oinks.

O the bard is sure he loves the moon. And the inanimate moon
loves him back with silences, and moonbeams made of chalk.

LXIII

O well, it was the night of the terrible jackhammer
and she put my exhausted pelt in the closet for a souvenir.

Baalim. Why can only one in seven be saved from them
and live again? They never come in fire but in perfect cold.

Sepulchral pussy. Annabel Lee of the snows—the night's
too long this time of year to sleep through. Dark edges.

All these songs may be sung to the kazoo and I am not
ashamed, add mongrels' bark, and the music of duck and pig.

Mab has returned as a giantess. She's out there bombs in
fist and false laurel, dressed anti-green in black metal.

From this vantage point I can only think of you in the
barnyard, one-tenth ounce panties and it's a good vision.

LXIV

That the housefly is guided in flight by a fly brain diminishes
me—there was a time when I didn't own such thoughts.

You admit then you wouldn't love me if I were a dog or rabbit,
was legless with truly bad skin. I have no defense. Same to you.

Poetry (that afternoon, of course) came flying through the
treetops, a shuddering pink bird, beshitting itself in flight.

When we were in love in 1956 I thought I would give up Keats
and be in the UAW and you would spend Friday's check wisely.

Hard rock, acid rock, goof balls, hash, haven't altered my love
for woodcock and grouse. It is the other way around, Mom.

I resigned. Walked down the steps. Got on the Greyhound bus
and went home only to find it wasn't what I remembered at all.

LXV

There was a peculiar faint light from low in the East
and a leaf skein that scattered it on the ground where I lay.

I fell into the hidden mine shaft in Keewanaw, emerging
in a year with teeth and eyes of burnished copper, black skin.

What will become of her, what will become of her now that
she's sold into slavery to an Air Force lieutenant?

I spent the night prophesying to the huge black rock
in the river around which the current boiled and slid.

We'll have to put a stop to this dying everywhere of young
men. It's not working out and they won't come back.

Those poems you wrote won't raise the dead or stir the
living or open the young girl's lips to jubilance.

from

LETTERS TO
YESENIN

to D.G.

This matted and glossy photo of Yesenin
bought at a Leningrad newsstand—permanently
tilted on my desk: he doesn't stare at me
he stares at nothing; the difference between
a plane crash and a noose adds up to nothing.
And what can I do with heroes with my brain fixed
on so few of them? Again nothing. Regard his flat
magazine eyes with my half-cocked own, both
of us seeing nothing. In the vodka was nothing
and Isadora was nothing, the pistol waved
in New York was nothing, and that plank bridge
near your village home in Ryazan covered seven feet
of nothing, the clumsy noose that swung the tilted
body was nothing but a noose, a law of gravity
this seeking for the ground, a few feet of nothing
between shoes and the floor a light year away.
So this is a song of Yesenin's noose which came
to nothing, but did a good job as we say back home
where there's nothing but snow. But I stood under
your balcony in St. Petersburg, yes St. Petersburg!
a crazed tourist with so much nothing in my heart
it wanted to implode. And I walked down to the Neva
embankment with a fine sleet falling and there was
finally something, a great river vastly flowing, flat
as your eyes; something to marry to my nothing heart
other than the poems you hurled into nothing those
years before the articulate noose.

2

I don't have any medals. I feel their lack
of weight on my chest. Years ago I was ambitious.
But now it is clear that nothing will happen.
All those poems that made me soar along a foot
from the ground are not so much forgotten as never
read in the first place. They rolled like moons
of light into a puddle and were drowned. Not even
the puddle can be located now. Yet I am encouraged
by the way you hung yourself, telling me that such
things don't matter. You, the fabulous poet of
Mother Russia. But still, even now, school girls
hold your dead heart, your poems, in their laps
on hot August afternoons by the river while they wait
for their boyfriends to get out of work or their
lovers to return from the army, their dead pets to
return to life again. To be called to supper. You
have a new life on their laps and can scent their
lavender scent, the cloud of hair that falls
over you, feel their feet trailing in the river,
or hidden in a purse walk the Neva again. Best of all
you are used badly like a bouquet of flowers to make
them shed their dresses in apartments. See those
steam pipes running along the ceiling. The rope.

I wanted to feel exalted so I picked up
Dr. Zhivago again. But the newspaper was there
with the horrors of the Olympics, those dead and
perpetually martyred sons of David. I want to present
all Israelis with .357 magnums so that they are
never to be martyred again. I wanted to be exalted
so I picked up *Dr. Zhivago* again but the TV was on
with a movie about the sufferings of convicts in
the early history of Australia. But then the movie
was over and the level of the bourbon bottle was dropping
and I still wanted to be exalted lying there with
the book on my chest. I recalled Moscow but I could
not place dear Yuri, only you Yesenin, seeing the Kremlin
glitter and ripple like Asia. And when drunk you appeared
as some Bakst stage drawing, a slain tartar. But that is
all ballet. And what a dance you had kicking your legs from
the rope—we all change our minds Berryman said in Minnesota
halfway down the river. Villon said of the rope that my neck
will feel the weight of my ass. But I wanted to feel exalted
again and read the poems at the end of *Dr. Zhivago* and
just barely made it. Suicide. Beauty takes my courage
away this cold autumn evening. My year old daughter's red
robe hangs from the doorknob shouting stop.

4

I am four years older than you but scarcely an unwobbling
pivot. It was no fun sitting around being famous, was it?
I'll never have to learn that lesson. You find a page torn
out of a book and read it feeling that here you might find
the mystery of print in such phrases as "summer was on the
way" or "Gertrude regarded him somewhat quizzically." Your
Sagane was a fraud. Love poems to girls you never met living
in a country you never visited. I've been everywhere to no
particular purpose. And am well past love but not love poems.
I wanted to fall in love on the coast of Ecuador but the girls
were itsy-bitsy and showers are not prominent in that area.
Unlike Killarney where I also didn't fall in love the girls
had good teeth. As in the movies the latin girls proved to be
spitfires with an endemic shanker problem. I didn't fall in love
in Palm Beach or Paris. Or London. Or Leningrad. I wanted to fall
in love at the ballet but my seat was too far back to see faces
clearly. At Sadko a pretty girl was sitting with a general
and did not exchange my glance. In Normandy I fell in love but
had colitis and couldn't concentrate. She had a way of not paying
any attention to me that could not be misunderstood. That is
a year's love story. Except Key West where absolutely nothing
happened with romantic overtones. Now you might understand why
I drink and grow fat. When I reach three hundred pounds there
will be no more love problems, only fat problems. Then I will
write reams of love poems. And if she pats my back a cubic yard
of fat will jiggle. Last night I drank a hundred proof quart
and looked at a photo of my sister. Ten years dead. Show me a
single wound on earth that love has healed. I fed my dying dog
a pound of beef and buried her happy in the barnyard.

5

Lustra. Officially the cold comes from Manitoba;
yesterday at sixty knots. So that the waves mounted
the breakwater. The first snow. The farmers and carpenters
in the tavern with red, wind burned faces. I am in there
playing the pinball machine watching all those delicious
lights flutter, the bells ring. I am halfway through
a bottle of vodka and am happy to hear Manitoba
howling outside. Home for dinner I ask my baby daughter
if she loves me but she is too young to talk. She cares
most about eating as I care most about drinking. Our wants
are simple as they say. Still when I wake from my nap
the universe is dissolved in grief again. The baby is sleeping
and I have no one to talk my language. My breath is shallow
and my temples pound. Vodka. Last October in Moscow I taught
a group of East Germans to sing "Fuck Nixon," and we were
quite happy until the bar closed. At the newsstand I saw a
picture of Bella Ahkmadulina and wept. Vodka. You would have
liked her verse. The doorman drew near, alarmed. Outside
the KGB floated through the snow like arctic bats.
Maybe I belong there. They won't let me print my verses. On the
night train to Leningrad I will confess everything to someone.
All my books are remaindered and out of print. My face in
the mirror asks me who I am and says I don't know. But stop
this whining. I am alive and a hundred thousand acres of birches
around my house wave in the wind. They are women standing
on their heads. Their leaves on the ground today are small
saucers of snow from which I drink with endless thirst.

6

Fruit and butter. She smelled like the skin of an apple.
The sun was hot and I felt an unbounded sickness with earth.
A single October day began to last a year. You can't fuck
your life away I thought. But you can! Listening in Nepal
to those peahens scream in the evening. Then through the glade
lordly he enters, his ass a ten foot fan, a painting by a crazed
old master. Look, they are human. Heads the size of two knuckles.
But returning to her buttery appleness and autumn, my dead friend.
We cannot give our lives over to women. Kneeling there under that
vulgar sugar maple tree I couldn't breathe and with a hundred
variations of red above me and against my mouth. She said I'm
going away to Oregon perhaps. I said that I'm going myself to
California where I hear they sleep out every night. So that
ended that and the fan was tucked neatly and the peahens' screams
were heard no more in the land and old ladies and old men slept
soundly again and threw away their cotton earplugs and the earth
of course was soaked with salt and August passed without a single
ear of corn. Of course this was only one neighborhood. Universality
is disgusting. But you had your own truly insurmountable horrors
with that dancer, lacking all wisdom as you did. Your critic said
you were "often revolted by your sensuality." He means
all of that endless fucking of course. Tsk tsk. Put one measure
against another and how rarely they fuse, and how almost never is
there any fire and how often there is only boredom and a craving
for cigarettes, a sandwich, or a drink. Particularly a drink.
I am drunk because I no longer can love. I make love and I'm
writing on a blackboard. Once it was a toteboard, a gun handle
until I myself became a notch. And a notch, to be obvious, is a
nothing. This all must pass as a monk's tale, a future lie.

Death thou comest when I had thee least in mind said Everyman
years ago in England. Can't get around much anymore. So it's
really a terrible surprise unless like you we commit suicide.
I worry some that the rope didn't break your neck, but that
you dangled there strangling from your body's weight. Such
physics can mean a rather important matter of three or four
minutes. Then I would guess there was a moment of black peacefulness
then you were hurtling in space like a mortar. Who can say
if a carcass smiles, if the baggage is happy at full rest. The
child drowns in a predictable puddle or inside the plastic bag
from which you just took your tuxedo. The evening is certainly
ruined and we can go on from there but that too is predictable.
I want to know. I have no explanations for myself but if someone
told me that my sister wasn't with Jesus they would get an
ass-kicking. There's a fascinating tumor called a melanoma
that apparently draws pigment from surrounding tissue until
it's black as coal. That fatal lump of coal tucked against the
spine. And of all things on earth a bullet can hit human
flesh is one of the least resistant. It's late autumn and this
is an official autumnal mood, a fully sanctioned event in which
one may feel the thrill of victory and the agony of defeat. But
as poets we would prefer to have a star fall on us, (that meteor
got me in the gizzard!), or lightning strike us and not while we're
playing golf but perhaps out in a wheatfield while we're making
love in a thunderstorm, or a tornado take us away outside of
Mingo, Kansas, like Judy Garland unfortunately. Or a rainbow
suffocate us. Or skewered dueling the mighty forces of anti-
art. Maybe in sleep as a Grey Eminence. A painless sleep of course.
Or saving a girl from drowning who turns out to be a mermaid.

8

I cleaned the granary dust off your photo with my shirt-sleeve.
Now that we are tidy we can wait for the host to descend
presumably from the sky as that seems to exhaust the alternatives.
You had a nice summer in the granary. I was out there with you
every day in June and July writing one of my six-week wonders,
another novel. Loud country music on the phonograph, wasps
and bees and birds and mice. The horses looked in the window
every hour or so, curious and rather stupid. Chief Joseph stared
down from the wall at both of us, a far nobler man than
we ever thought possible. We can't lead ourselves and he led
a thousand with a thousand horses a thousand miles. He was a god
and had three wives when one is usually more than enough for
a human. These past weeks I have been organizing myself into
my separate pieces. I have the limberness of a man twice my age
and this is as good a time as any to turn around. Joseph was
very understanding, incidentally, when the Cavalry shot so many
of the women and children. It was to be expected. Earth is
full of precedents. They hang around like underground trees
waiting for their chance. The fish swam for four years solid
in preparation for August the seventh, 1972, when I took his life
and ate his body. Just as we may see our own ghosts next to
us whose shapes we will someday flesh out. All of this suffering
to become a ghost. Yours held a rope, Manila, straight from
the tropics. But we don't reduce such glories to a mudbath.
The ghost giggles at genuflections. You can't buy him a drink.
Out in a clearing in the woods the other day I got up on a
stump and did a little dance for mine. We know the most fright-
ening time is noon. The evidence says I'm half way there, such
wealth I can't give away, thirty-four years of seconds.

What if I own more paper clips than I'll ever use in this
lifetime. My other possessions are shabby: the house half
painted, the car without a muffler, one dog with bad eyes
and the other dog a horny moron. Even the baby has a rash on
her neck but then we don't own humans. My good books were
stolen at parties long ago and two of the barn windows are
broken and the furnace is unreliable and field mice daily
feed on the wiring. But the new foal appears healthy though
unmanageable, crawling under the fence and chased by my wife
who is stricken by the flu, not to speak of my own body which
has long suffered the ravages of drink and various nervous
disorders which make me laugh and weep and caress my shotguns.
But paper clips. Rich in paper clips to sort my writings which
fill so many cartons under the bed. When I attach them I say
it's your job after all to keep this whole thing together. And
I used them once with a rubberband to fire holes into the
face of the president hanging on the office wall. We have freedom.
You couldn't do that to Brezhnev much less Stalin on whose
grave Mandelstam sits proudly in the form of the ultimate
crow, a peerless crow, a crow without comparison on earth.
But the paper clips are a small comfort like meeting someone
fatter than myself and we both wordlessly recognize the fact
or meeting someone my age who is more of a drunk, more savaged
and hag ridden until they are no longer human and seeing
them on the street I wonder how their heads which are only
wounds balance on the top of their bodies. A manuscript of
a novel sits in front of me held together with twenty clips.
It is the paper equivalent of a duck and a company far away
has bought this perhaps beautiful duck and my time is free again.

It would surely be known for years after as the day I shot
a cow. Walking out of the house before dawn with the sky an icy
blackness and not one star or cockcrow or shiver of breeze, the rifle
barrel black and icy to the touch. I walked a mile in the dark
and a flushed grouse rose louder than any thunderclap. I entered
a neck of a woodlot I'd scouted and sat on a stump waiting for
a deer I intended to kill. But then I was dressed too warmly
and had a formidable hangover with maybe three hours of sleep so
I slept again seeing a tin open-fronted café in Anconcito down
on the coast of Ecuador and the eyes of a piglet staring at me as
I drank my mineral water dazed with the opium I had taken for
la turista. Crippled syphilitic children begging, one little boy
with a tooth as long as a forefinger, an ivory tusk which would
be pulled on maturity and threaded as an amulet ending up finally
in Moscow in a diplomatic pouch. The boy would explore with his
tongue the gum hole for this Russian gift. What did he know about
Russia. Then carrying a naked girl in the water on my shoulders
and her shorthairs tickled the back of my neck with just the suggestion
of a firm grip behind them so if I had been stupid enough to turn
around I might have suffocated at eighteen and not written you
any letters. There were bristles against my neck and hot breath
in my hair. It must be a deer smelling my hair so I wheeled and shot.
But it was a cow and the muzzle blast was blue in the grey light.
She bawled horribly and ran in zigzags. I put her away with a shot
to the head. What will I do with this cow? It's a guernsey and she
won't be milked this morning. I knelt and stared into her huge eyeball,
her iris making a mirror so I combed my hair and thought about the
whole dreary mess. Then I walked backward through a muddy orchard
so I wouldn't be trailed, got in my car and drove to New York nonstop.

1 1

for Diane W.

No tranquil pills this year wanting to live peeled as they
described the nine throats of Cerebus. Those old greek names
keep popping up. You can tell we went to college and our sleep
is troubled. There are geographical equivalents for exotic tropes
of mind; living peeled was the Desert Inn in Tucson talking with D. W.
about love and art with so much pain my ears rung and the breath
came short. And outside the fine desert air wasn't fine anymore:
the indians became kachina dolls and a girl was tortured daily
for particular reasons. This other is our Akhmatova and often we want
to hide from her—seasoned as she is in so many hells. But why paint
her for one of the dead who knew her pungency of love, the unforgivable
low tide smell of it, how few of us bear it for long before reducing
it to a civil act. You were odd for a poet attaching yourself
to a woman no less a poet than yourself. It still starts with
the dance. In the end she probably strangled you and maybe back
in Ryazan there was a far better bird with less extravagant plumage.
But to say I'm going to spend the day thinking wisely about
women is to say I'm going to write an indomitably great poem before
lunch or maybe rule the world by tomorrow dawn. And I couldn't
love one of those great SHES—it's far too late and they are far
too few to find anyway though that's a driveling excuse. I saw one
in a tree and on a roof. I saw one in a hammock and thigh deep
in a pond. I saw one out in the desert and sitting under a willow
by the river. All past tense you notice and past haunting but not
past caring. What did she do to you and did you think of her when
your terrible shadow fell down the wall. I see that creature sitting
on the lawn in Louvicienne, the mistress of a superior secret. We
have both died from want of her, cut off well past our prime.

12

I was proud at four that my father called me Little Turd of Misery.
A special name somehow connected to all the cows and horses in
the perpetual mire of the barnyard. It has a resonance to it un-
known to president senator poet septic-tank cleaner critic butcher
hack or baker liberal or snot, rightist and faker and faggot and
cunt hound. A child was brought forth and he was named Little Turd
of Misery and like you was thrown into the lake to learn how to
swim, owned dogs that died stupidly but without grief. Why does
the dog chase his broken legs in a circle. He almost catches them
like we almost catch our unruly poems. And our fathers and uncles
had ordinary pursuits, hunted and fished, smelled of tobacco and
liquor, grew crops, made sauerkraut and wine, wept in the dark,
chased stray cows, mended fences, were hounded as they say by
creditors. Barns burned. Cabbages rotted. Corn died of drought
before its holy ears were formed, wheat flattened by hail and wind and
the soup grew only one potato and a piece of salt pork from its
center. Generations of slavery. All so we could fuck neurotically
and begin the day rather than end it drinking and dreaming of dead
dogs, swollen creeks with small bridges, ponds where cows are caught
and drown sucked in by the muck. But the wary boy catches fish
there, steals a chicken for his dog's monthly birthday, learns
to smoke, sees his first dirty picture and sings his first dirty
song, goes away, becomes deaf with song, becomes blinded by love,
gets letters from home but never returns. And his nights become less black
and holy, less moon blown and sweet. His brain burns away like
gray paraffin. He's tired. His parents are dead or he is dead
to his parents. He smells the smell of a horse. The room is
cold. He dims the light and builds a noose. It works too well.

[138]

All of those little five dollar a week rooms smelling thick of
cigarette smoke and stale tea bags. The private bar of soap
smearing the dresser top, on the chair a box of cookies and a letter
from home. And what does he think he's doing and do we all begin our
voyage into Egypt this way. The endless bondage of words. That's why
you turned to those hooligan taverns and vodka, Crane to his
sailors in Red Hook. Four walls breathe in and out. The clothes on
the floor are a dirty shroud. The water is stale in its glass.
Just one pull on the bottle starts the morning faster. If you
don't rouse your soul you will surely die while others are having
lunch. Noon. You passed the point of retreat and took that dancer,
a goad, perhaps a goddess. The food got better anyhow and the
bottles. This is all called romantic by some without nostrils
tinctured by cocaine. No romance here, but a willingness to age
and die at the speed of sound. Outside there's a successful revolution
and you've been designated a parasite. Everywhere crushed women
are bearing officious anti-semites. Stalin begins his diet of
iron shavings and blood. Murder swings with St. Basil's bell, a
thousand per gong free of charge. North on the Baltic Petrodvorets
is empty and inland, Pushkin is empty. Nabokov has sensibly flown
the shabby coop. But a hundred million serfs are free and own
more than the common bread; a red-tinged glory, neither fire nor
sun, a sheen without irony on the land. Who could care that you
wanted to die, that your politics changed daily, that your songs
turned to glass and were broken. No time to marry back in Ryazan
buy a goat, three dogs, and fish for perch. The age gave you a
pistol and you gave it back, gave you two wives and you gave
them both back, gave you a rope to swing from which you used wisely.
You were good enough to write that last poem in blood.

Imagine being a dog and never knowing what you're doing. You're
simply *doing:* eating garbage, fawning, mounting in public with
terrible energy. But let's not be romantic. Those curs, however
sweet, don't have souls. For all of the horrors at least some of
us have better lives than dogs. Show me a dog that ever printed
a book of poems read by no one in particular before he died at
seventeen, old age for a dog. No dog ever equaled Rimbaud for
grace or greatness, for rum running, gun running, slave trading
and buggery. The current phrase "anything that gets you off"
includes dogs but they lack our catholicity. Still Sergei we never
wanted to be dogs. Maybe indians or princes, caesars or mongolian
chieftains, women in expensive undergarments. But if women, lesbians
to satisfy our ordinary tastes for women. In a fantasy if you
become a woman you quickly are caressing your girlfriend. That
pervert. I never thought she would. Be like that. When she's away
from me. Back to consciousness, the room smells like a locker room.
Out the window it's barely May in Moscow and the girls have shed
their winter coats. One watches a group of fishermen. She has
green eyes and is recent from the bath. If you were close enough
which you'll never be you could catch her scent of lemon and
the clear softness of her nape where it meets her hair. She'll
probably die of flu next year or marry an engineer. The same
things really as far as you're concerned. And it's the same in this
country. A fine wife and farm, children, animals, three good reviews.
Then a foggy day in late March with dozens of crows in the air
and a girl on a horse passes you in the woods. Your dog barks.
The girl stops, laughing. She has green eyes. Your heart is off
and running. Your groin hopes. You pray not to see her again.

The soul of water. The most involved play. She wonders if she
is permitted to name the stars. Tell her no. This month, May,
is said to be "the month of tiny plant-sucking pests." So even
nature is said to war against us though those pests it seems are
only having lunch. So the old woman had named the stars above
her hut and wondered if god had perhaps given them other names that
she didn't know about. Her priest was always combing his hair
and shining his shoes. We were driven from the church, weren't we
Sergei? In hearses. But is this time for joking? Yes. Always.
We wonder if our fathers in heaven or hell watch when we are about
our lying and shameful acts. As if they up or down there weren't
sick enough of life without watching for eternity some faulty
version of it, no doubt on a kind of TV. Tune the next hour out
dad, I'm going to be bad. Six lines of coke and a moronic twitch.
Please don't watch. I can't help myself. I provide for my children.
They're delighted with the fish I catch. My wife smiles hourly.
She has her horses, dogs, cat, barn, garden. But in New York twenty
layers above the city some cloud or stratum of evil wants to enter
me and I'm certainly willing. Even on ground level in Key West.
Look she has no clothes on and I only wanted to be a friend and
maybe talk about art. Only a lamb. Of course this Little Boy Blue
act is tiresome and believed by no one on earth, heaven or hell.
So we've tried to name the stars and think we are forgiven in
advance. Rimbaud turned to black or arab boys remembering when he
was twelve and there was no evil. Only a helpless sensual wonder.
Pleasure gives. And takes. It is dark and hot and the brain is
howling with those senseless drugs. Mosquitoes land upon those
fields of sweat, the pool between her breasts. You want to be home
rocking your child in a sunny room. Now that it's over. But wait.

Today we've moved back to the granary again and I've anointed
the room with *Petrouchka*. Your story, I think. And music. That
ends with you floating far above in St. Petersburg's blue winter
air, shaking your fist among the fish and green horses, the dim-
inuitive yellow sun and chicken playing the bass drum. Your
sawdust is spilled and you are forever borne by air. A simple story.
Another madman, Nijinsky, danced your part and you danced his.
None of us apparently is unique. Think of dying waving a fist full
of ballpoint pens that change into small snakes and that your
skull will be transposed into the cymbal it was always meant to be.
But shall we come down to earth? For years I have been too ready
to come down to earth. A good poet is only a sorcerer bored with
magic who has turned his attention elsewhere. O let us see wonders
that psilocybin never conceived of in her powdery head. Just now
I stepped on a leaf that blew in the door. There was a buzzing
and I thought it concealed a wasp, but the dead wasp turned out to be
a tiny bird, smaller than a hummingbird or june bug. Probably one
of a kind and I can tell no one because it would anger the swarm
of naturalists so vocal these days. I'll tuck the body in my hair
where it will remain forever a secret or tape it to the back of
your picture to give you more depth than any mirror on earth.
And another oddity: the record needle stuck just at the point
the trumpet blast announced the appearance of your ghost in the
form of Petrouchka. I will let it repeat itself a thousand times
through the afternoon until you stand beside the desk in your
costume. But I've no right to bring you back to life. We must
respect your affection for the rope. You knew the exact juncture
in your life that the act of dangling could be made a dance.

Behind my back I have returned to life with much more surprise
than conviction. All those months in the cold with neither
tears nor appetite no matter that I was in Nairobi or Arusha, Rome,
the fabled Paris flat and dry as a newsphoto. And lions looked
like lions in books. Only the rumbling sound of an elephant shooting
water into his stomach with a massive trunk made any sense. But I
thought you would have been pleased with the Galla women in Ethiopia
and walking the Colonnade near the Vendôme I knew you had walked
there. Such a few signs of life. Life brings us down to earth he
thinks. Father of two at thirty-five can't seem to earn a living.
But whatever muse there is on earth is not concerned with groceries.
We like to believe that Getty couldn't buy a good line for a billion
dollars. When we first offered ourselves up to her when young and
in our waking dreams she promised nothing. Not certainly that we
could buy a bike for our daughter's birthday or eat good cuts of
beef instead of hamburger. She doesn't seem to care that our wine
is ordinary. She walks in and out the door without knocking. She takes
off her clothes and ruins the marriage bed. She out and out killed
you Sergei for no reason I can think of. And you might want to
kill her but she changes so fast whether into a song, a deer, a pig,
the girl sitting on the pier in a short dress. You want to fish
but you turn and there larger than any movie are two thighs and louder
than any howl they beckon you to the life they hold so gently. We
said that her eyes were bees and ice glistened in her hair. And we
know she can become a rope but then you're never sure as all rope
tends to resemble itself though it is common for it to rest in coils
like snakes. Or rope. But I must earn our living and can't think
about rope though I am to be allowed an occasional girl drawing up
her thighs on a pier. You might want her even in your ghostly form.

Thus the poet is a beached gypsy, the first porpoise to whom it
occurred to commit suicide. True, my friend, even porpoises have
learned your trick and for similar reasons: losing hundreds of
thousands of wives, sons, daughters, husbands to the tuna nets.
The seventh lover in a row disappears and it can't be endured.
There is some interesting evidence that Joplin was a porpoise and
simply decided to stop breathing at an unknown depth. Perhaps the
navy has her body and is exploring ways to turn it into a weapon.
Off Boca Grande a baby porpoise approached my boat. It was a girl
about the size of my two year old daughter who might for all I know
be a porpoise. Anyway she danced around the boat for an hour
while her mother kept a safer distance. I set the mother at ease by
singing my infamous theme song: "Death dupe dear dingle devil flower
bird dung girl," repeating seven times until the mother approached
and I leaned over the gunnel and we kissed. I was tempted to swim
off with them but remembered I had a date with someone who tripled
as a girl, cocaine dealer and duck though she chose to be the last,
alas, that evening. And as in all ancient stories I returned to the
spot but never found her or her little girl again. Even now mariners
passing the spot deep in the night can hear nothing. But enough
of porpoise love. And how they are known to beach themselves. I've
begun to doubt whether we ever would have been friends. Maybe. Not
that it's to the point—I know three one-eyed poets like myself
but am close to none of them. These letters might have kept me
alive—something to do you know as opposed to the nothing you chose.
Loud yeses don't convince. Nietzsche said you were a rope dancer
before you were born. I say yes before breakfast but to the smell
of bacon. Wise souls move through the dark only one step at a time.

19

Naturally we would prefer seven epiphanies a day and an earth
not so apparently devoid of angels. We become very tired with
pretending we like to earn a living, with the ordinary objects and
events of our lives. What a beautiful toothbrush. How wonderful
to work overtime. What a nice cold we have to go with the cold
crabbed spring. How fun to have no money at all. This thin soup
tastes great. I'm learning something every morning from cheap wine
hangovers. These rejection slips are making me a bigger person.
The mailbox is always so empty let's paint it pink. It's good for
my soul that she prefers to screw another. Our cat's right eyeball
became ulcerated and had to be pulled but she's the same old cat.
I can't pay my taxes and will be sent to prison but it will probably
be a good experience. That rattlesnake striking at dog and daughter
was interesting. How it writhed beautifully with its head cut
off and dog and daughter were tugging at it. How purging to lose
our last twenty dollars in a crap game. Seven come eleven indeed.
But what grand songs you made out of an awful life though you had
no faith that less was more, that there was some golden splendor
in humiliation. After all those poems you were declared a coward
and a parasite. Mayakovsky hissed in public over your corpse and
work only to take his own life a little while later. Meanwhile
back in America Crane had his Guggenheim year and technically jumped
ship. Had he been seven hundred feet tall he would have been OK.
I suspect you would have been the kind of friends you both needed
so badly. So many husbands have little time for their homosexual
friends. But we should never imagine we love this daily plate of shit.
The horses in the yard bite and chase each other. I'll make a carol
of my dream: carried in a litter by lovely women, a 20 lb. bag of cocaine,
angels shedding tunics in my path, all dead friends come to life again.

The mushrooms helped again: walking hangdoggedly to the granary
after the empty mailbox trip I saw across the barnyard at the base
of an elm stump a hundred feet away a group of white morels. How
many there were will be kept concealed for obvious reasons. While
I plucked them I considered each a letter from the outside world
to my little cul de sac, this valley: catching myself in this act
doing what I most despise, throwing myself in the laps of others.
Save my life. Help me. By return post. That sort of thing. So we
throw ourselves in the laps of others until certain famous laps
grow tired, vigorous laps whose movement is slowed by the freight
of all those cries. Then if you become famous after getting off
so many laps you can look at the beautiful women at your feet and
say I'll take that foot and that breast and that thigh and those lips
you have become so denatured and particular. They float and merge
their parts trying to come up with something that will please you.
Selecting the finest belly you write your name with a long thin
line of cocaine but she is perspiring and you can't properly snort
it off. Disappointments. The belly weeps but you dismiss her, sad
and frightened that your dreams have come to no end. Why cast Robert
Redford in your life story if all that he's going to do is sit there
and piss and moan at the typewriter for two hours in expensive
Eastman color. Not much will happen if you don't like to drink
champagne out of shoes. And sated with a half dozen French meals a day
you long for those simple boiled potatoes your estranged wife made
so perfectly. The letters from your children are defiled in a stack
of fan mail and obscene photos. Your old dog and horse have been
given to kindly people and your wife will soon marry a jolly farmer.
No matter that your million selling books are cast in bronze. On a
whim you fly to Palm Beach, jump on your yacht and set the automatic.
You fit a nylon hawser around your neck, hurl overboard, and after
the sharks have lunch your head skips in the noose like a marlin bait.

To answer some of the questions you might ask were you alive and
had we become friends but what do poets ask one another after long
absence? How have you been other than dead and how have I been
dying on earth without naming the average string of complaints which
is only worrying aloud, naming the dreaded motes that float around
the brain, those pink balloons calling themselves poverty, failure,
sickness, lust, and envy. To mention a very few. But you want part-
iculars, not the human condition or a letter to the editor on why
when I'm at my worst I think I've been fucked over. So here's this
spring's news: now that the grass is taller I walk in some fear of
snakes. Feeling melancholy I watched my wife plant the garden row
on row while the baby tried to catch frogs. It's hard not to eat too
much when you deeply love food but I've limited myself to a half
gallon of burgundy a day. On long walks my eyes are so sunk back
in my brain they see nothing, then move forward again toward the light
and see a high meadow turning pale green and swimming in the fog
with crows tracing perceptible and geometrical paths just above
the fog but audible. At the shore I cast for fish, some of them
large with deliquescing smelt and alewives in their bellies. Other
than marriage I haven't been in love for years; close calls over
the world I mentioned to you before, but it's not love if it isn't
a surprise. I look at women and know deeply they are from another
planet and sometimes even lightly touching a girl's arm I know
I am touching a lovely though alien creature. We don't get back
those days we don't caress, don't make love. If I could get you out
in the backcountry down in Key West and get some psilocybin into
you you would cut your legendary vodka consumption. Naturally I
still believe in miracles and the holy fate of the imagination. How
is it being dead and would I like it and should I put it off for a while?

These last few notes to you have been a bit somber like biographies
of artists written by joyless people so that the whole book is
a record of agony at thirty rather than thirty-three and a third.
You know the sound—Keeeaaattts wuzzzz verrrry unhapppppppy abouttt
dyinnnng. So here are some of those off the wall extravagancies.
Dawn in Ecuador with mariachi music, dawn at Ngorongoro with elephant
far below in the crater swagging through the marsh grass, dawn in
Moscow and snowing with gold minarets shouting that you have at last
reached Asia, dawn in Addis Ababa with a muslim waver in the cool
air smelling of ginger and a lion roaring on the lawn, dawn in
bleery Paris with a roll tasting like zinc and a girl in a cellophane
blouse staring at you with four miraculous eyes, dawn in Normandy
with a conceivable princess breathing in the next room and horses
wandering across the moat beneath my window, dawn in Montana with
herons calling from the swamp, dawn in Key West wondering if it was
a woman or tarpon that left your bed before cockcrow, dawn at home
when your eyes are molten and the ghost of your dog chases the fox
across the pasture, dawn on the Escanaba with trout dimpling the
mist and the water with a dulcet roar, dawn in London when the party
girl leaves your taxi to go home to Shakespeare, dawn in Leningrad
with the last linden leaves falling and you knocking at the door
for a drunken talk but I am asleep. Not to speak of the endless and
nearly unconscious water walks after midnight when even the stars
might descend another foot to get closer to earth. Heat. The wetness
of air. Couplings. Even the mosquitoes are lovely and seem to imitate
miniature birds. And a lion's cough is followed rhythmically by a
hyena's laugh to prove that nature loves symmetry. The black girl
leaves the grand hotel for her implausibly shabby home. The poet
had dropped five sorts of drugs in his belly swill of alcohol and
has imagined his deathless lines commemorating your last Leningrad night.

23

I want to bother you with some recent nonsense; a classmate dropped
dead, his heart was attacked at thirty-three. At the crematory
they lowered his body by fire-resistant titanium cables reminding
one of the steak on a neglected barbecue grill only more so. We're
not supposed to believe that the vase of ashes is the real him.
You can imagine the mighty roar of the gas jets, a train coming
closer, the soul of thunder. But this is only old hat, or old death,
whichever. "Pause here, son of sorrow, remember death," someone once
said. "We can't have all things here to please us, our little Sue Ann
is gone to Jesus," reads an Alabama gravestone. But maybe even Robert
Frost or Charles Olson don't know they are dead. That would include
you of course. It is no quantity, absolute zero, the air in a hole
minus its airiness, the vacuum from the passing bird or bullet, the
end of the stem where the peach was, the place above the ground
where the barn burned with such energy we plugged our ears. If not,
show yourself in ten minutes. Let's settle this issue because I feel
badly today: a sense that my teeth and body are rotting on the hoof.
I could avoid the whole thing with a few drinks—it's been over
eight hours—but I want to face it like Simon Magus or poor Faustus.
Nothing, however, presents itself other than that fading picture of
my sister with an engine in her lap, not a very encouraging item
to be sure. I took Anna who is two for her first swim today. We didn't
know we were going swimming so she wore a pink dress, standing in
the lake up to her waist in wonderment. The gaucheries of children,
the way they love birds and neon lights, kill snakes and eat sand.
But I decided I wanted to go swimming for the first time and wanted
to make love for the first time again. These thoughts can make you
unhappy. Perhaps if your old dog had been in the apartment that night
you wouldn't have done it. Everything's so fragile except ropes.

Dear friend. It rained long and hard after a hot week and when I
awoke the world was green and leafy again, or as JD says, everything
was new like a warm rain after a movie. And I said enough of death
and its obvious health hazards, it's a white on white jig saw puzzle
in one piece. An hour with the doctor yesterday when he said my
blood pressure was so high I might explode as if I had just swallowed
an especially tasty grenade. I must warn my friends not to stand
too close. Blood can be poisonous; the Kikuyu in Kenya are often
infected when they burrow hacking away in the gut of an elephant.
Some don't come back. But doctors don't say such things, except
W. C. Williams. Just like your doctor when you were going batty mine
said "you must be distressed, you eat and drink and smoke far too
much. Cut out these things. The lab found lilacs and part of the
backbone of a garter snake or garter in your stool sample, and the
remnants of a hair ball. Do you chew your comb? We are checking to
see if it's your hair as there are possible criminal questions here.
Meanwhile get this thatch of expensive prescriptions filled and I
advise extensive psychiatric care. I heard your barking when I left
the room. How did you manage gout at your age?" My eyes misted
and I heard fiddle music and I looked up from page 86 in the June
Vogue where my old nemesis Lauren Hutton was staring at me in a
doctor's office in northern Michigan. This is Paul Bunyan country
Lauren. And how did I get gout? All of that fried salt and side
pork as a child. Humble fare. Quintuple heaps of caviar and decanters
of vodka at the Hotel Europa in Leningrad. *Tête de veau,* the brains,
tongue and cheeks of a calf. Side orders of *tripe à la mode de Caen*
sweetbreads with morels. Stewed kidneys and heart. Three pound steaks
as snacks, five dozen oysters and three lobsters in Boston. A barrel
of nice gravy. Wild boar. Venison. Duck. Partridge. Pig's feet. But
you know, Sergei, I must eat these magical trifles to keep from
getting brainy and sad, to avoid leaving this physical world.

An afterthought to my previous note; we must closely watch any self-pity and whining. It simply isn't manly. Better by far to be a cow-boy drinking rusty water, surviving on the maggots that unwittingly ate the pemmican in the saddlebags. I would be the Lone and I don't need no one said the cowpoke. Just a man and his horse against everything else on earth and horses are so dumb they run all day from flies never learning that flies are everywhere. Though in their violent motion they avoid the flies for a few moments. It's time again not to push a metaphor too far. But back again to the success-ful farmer who has his original hoe bronzed like baby shoes above the Formica mantelpiece—I earned what I got, nobody give me nothing he says. Pasternak said you probably didn't think death was the end of it all. Maybe you were only checking it out for something new to write about. We thieves of fire are capable of such arrogance when not otherwise occupied as real people pretending to be poet farmers, important writers, capable lovers, sports fops, regular guys, rock stars with tiny nonetheless appreciative audiences. But the self-pity and whining must stop. I forgot to add that at the doctor's an old woman called in to say that her legs had turned blue and she couldn't walk or hold her urine and she was alone. Try that one on. Thirty years ago I remember my mother singing hello Central, give me heaven, I think my daddy is there about the usual little boy in a wartime situation. We forget about those actual people, certainly our ancestors and neighbors, who die in earnest. They called my dad, the county agent, and his friend a poor farmer was swinging like you only from a rafter in the barn from a hay rope. What to do with his strange children—their thin bodies, low brows and narrow eyes— who were my schoolmates. They're working in auto factories now and still voiceless. We are different in that we suffer and love, are bored, with our mouths open and must speak on occasion for those others.

26

Going in the bar last Sunday night I noticed that they were having
high-school graduation down the street. Caps and gowns. June and
mayflies fresh from the channel fluttering in the warm still air.
After a few drinks I felt jealous and wanted someone to say "best of
luck in your chosen field," or "the road of life is ahead of you."
Remember your first trip to Moscow at nineteen? Everything was poss-
ible. You watched those noble women at the riding academy who would
soon be permanently unhorsed, something you were to have mixed
feelings about what with the way poets suck up to, are attracted
to the aristocracy however jimcrack. And though the great Blok
welcomed you, you felt tentative, an unknown quantity, and remained
so for several years. But how quickly one goes from being unknown
and embarrassed to bored and arrogant, from being ignored to expecting
deference. From fleabag rooms to at least the Plaza. And the daydreams
and hustling, the fantasies and endless work that get you from one
to the other, only to discover that you really want to go home. Start
over with a new deck. But back home all the animals are dead, the
friends have disappeared and the fields gone to weed. The fish
have flown from the creeks and ponds and the birds have all drowned
or gone to China. No one knows you—they have little time for poetry
in the country, or in the city for that matter except for the minis-
trations of a few friends. Your name bobs up like a halloween
apple and literature people have the vague feeling that they should read
you if they ever "catch up" on their reading. Once on a train I saw
a girl reading a book of mine but she was homely and I had a toothache
so I let the moment pass. What delicious notoriety. The journalist
said I looked like a brick layer or beer salesman, not being fashion-
ably slender. But lately the sun shines through, the sweet release
of flinging these lines at the dead, almost like my baby Anna throw-
ing grain to the horses a mile away, in the far corner of the pasture.

27

I won my wings! I got all A's! We bought fresh fruit! The toilet
broke! Thus my life draws fuel ineluctably from triumph. Manic,
rainy June slides into July and I am carefully dressing myself in
primary colors for happiness. When the summer solstice has passed
you know you're finally safe again. That midnight surely dates
the year. "Look to your romantic interests and business investments"
says the star hack in the newspapers. But what if you have neither?
Millions will be up to nothing. One of those pure empty days with
all of the presence of a hole in the ground. The stars have stolen
twenty-four hours and vengeance is out of the question. But I'm
a three-peckered purple goat if you were tied to any planet by your
cord. That is mischief, an inferior magic; pulling the lining out
of a top hat. You merely rolled on the ground moaning trying to pull
that mask off but it had grown into your face. "Such a price the
gods exact for song to become what we sing," said someone. If it
aches that badly you have to take the head off, narrow the neck to
a third its normal size, a practice known as hanging by gift of the
state or as a do it yourself project. But what I wonder about is your
velocity: ten years from Ryazan to Leningrad. A little more than
a decade, two years into your fifth seven and on out like a proton
in an accelerator. You simply fell off the edge of the world while
most of us are given circles, or hopefully, spirals. The new
territory had a wall which you went over and on the other side there
was something we weren't permitted to see. Everyone suspects it's
nothing. Time will tell. But how you preyed on, longed for, those
first ten years. We'll have to refuse that, however its freshness
in your hands. Romantic. Fatal. We learn to see with the child's
delight again or perish. We hope it was your vision you lost,
that before those final minutes you didn't find out something new.

O to use the word winged as in bird or victory or airplane for
the first time. Not for spirit though, yours or anyone else's
or the bird that flew errantly into the car radiator. Or for poems
that sink heavily to our stomachs like fried foods, the powerful
ones, visceral, as impure as the bodies they flaunt. Curious what
you paid for your cocaine to get winged. We know the price of
the poems, one body and soul net, one brain already tethered to the
dark, one ingenious leash never to hold a dog, two midwinter eyes
that lost their technicolor. Think what you missed. Mayakovsky's
pistol shot. The Siege of Leningrad. Crows feasting on all of those
frozen German eyes. Good Russian crows that earned a meal putting
up with all of that insufferable racket of war. Curious crows watching
midnight purges, wary of owls, and the girl in the green dress
on the ground before a line of soldiers. She and the crow exchange
pitiless glances. She flaps her arms but is not winged. Maybe
there is one ancient crow that remembers the Czarina's jeweled
sleigh, the ring of its small gold bells; and the sickly winged
horse in the cellar of the Winter Palace, product of a mad breeding
experiment for eventual escape, how it was dumped into the Neva
before the talons grew through the hoofs, the marvel of it lost
in the uproar of those days, the proof of it in the bones somewhere
on the floor of the Baltic delta. But we all get lost in the course
of empire which lacks the Brownian movement's stability. We count
on iron men to stick to their guns. Our governments are weapons
of exhaustion. Poems fly out of yellow windows at night with a stall
factor just under a foot, beneath our knees and the pre-fourth of
July corn in the garden. At least at that level radar can't detect
them and they're safe from State interference. We know perfectly
well you flapped your arms madly, unwinged but craving a little flight.

29

We're nearing the end of this homage that often resembles a
suicide note to a suicide. I didn't mean it that way but how
often our hands sneak up on our throats and catch us unaware.
What are you doing here we say. Don't squeeze so hard. The hands
inside the vodka bottle and on the accelerator, needles and coke-
sore noses. It's not very attractive, is it? But now there is rain
on the tin roof, the world outside is green and leafy with bluebirds
this morning dive-bombing drowning worms from a telephone wire,
the baby laughing as the dog eats the thirty-third snake of the
summer. And the bodies on the streets and beaches. Girl bottoms!
Holy. Tummies in the sun! Very probably holy. Peach evidence almost
struggling for air! A libidinal stew that calls us to life however
ancient and basal. May they plug their lovely ears with their big
toes. God surely loves them to make them look that way and can I
do less than He at least in this respect. As my humble country
father said in our first birds and bees talk so many years ago "That
thing ain't just to pee through." This vulgarity saves us as
certainly as our chauvinism. Just now in midafternoon I wanted
a tumbler of wine but John Calvin said "You got up at noon. No wine
until you get your work done. You haven't done your exercises to
suppress the gut the newspaper says women find most disgusting.
The fence isn't mended and the neighbor's cow keeps crawling through
in the night, stealing the fresh clover you are saving for Rachel
the mare when she drops her foal." So the wine bottle remains
corked and Calvin slips through the floor boards to the crawl space
where he spends all of his time hating his body. Would these concerns
have saved you? Two daughters and a wife. Children prop our rotting
bodies with cries of earn earn earn. On occasion we are kissed. So odd
in a single green month to go from the closest to so far from death.

30

The last and I'm shrinking from the coldness of your spirit: that
chill lurid air that surrounds great Lenin in his tomb as if we
had descended into a cloud to find on the catafalque a man who has
usurped nature, isn't dead any more than you or I are dead. Only
unlikely to meet and talk in our current forms. Today I couldn't
understand words so I scythed ragweed and goldenrod before it could
go to seed and multiply. I played with god imagining to hold his
obvious scythe that caught you, so unlike the others, aware and
cooperative. Is he glad to help if we're willing? A boring question
since we're so able and ingenious. Sappho's sparrows are always
telling us that love will save us, some *other* will arrive to draw
us cool water, lie down with us in our private darkness and make
us well. I think not. What a fabulous lie. We've disposed of sparrows
and god, the death of color, those who are dominated by noon and
the vision of night flowing in your ears and eyes and down your
throat. But we didn't mean to arrive at conclusions. Fifty years are
only a moment between this granary and a hanged man half the earth
away. You are ten years younger than my grandmother Hulda who still
sings Lutheran hymns and watches the Muskegon River flow. In whatever
we do, we do damage to ourselves; and in those first images there
were always cowboys or cossacks fighting at night, murdered animals
and girls never to be touched; dozing with head on your dog's chest
you understand breath and believe in golden cities where you will
live forever. And that fatal expectancy—not comprehending that we
like our poems are flowers for the void. In those last days you
wondered why they turned their faces. Any common soul knew you
had consented to death, the only possible blasphemy. I write to
you like some half-witted, less courageous brother, unwilling to tease
those ghosts you slept with faithfully until they cast you out.

POSTSCRIPT

At 8:12 A.M. all of the watches in the world are being wound.
Which is not quite the same thing as all of the guitars on earth
being tuned at midnight. Or that all suicides come after the mail-
man when all hope is gone. Before the mailman watches are wound,
windows looked through, shoes precisely tied, tooth care, the
attenuations of the hangover noted. Which is not the same as
the new moon after midnight or her bare feet stepping slowly toward
you and the snake easing himself from the ground for a meal.
The world is so necessary. Someone must execute stray dogs and
free the space they're taking up. I can see people walking down
Nevsky Prospect winding their watches before you were discovered
too far above ground, that mystical space that was somewhere
occupied by a stray dog or a girl in an asylum on her hands
and knees. A hanged face turns slowly from a plum to a lump of
coal. I'm winding my watch in antipathy. I see the cat racing
around the yard in a fantasy of threat. She's preparing for
eventualities. She prizes the only prize. But we aren't the cats
we once were thousands of years ago. You didn't die with the
dignity of an animal. Today you make me want to tie myself to
a tree, stake my feet to earth herself so I can't get away. It didn't
come as a burning bush or pillar of light but I've decided to stay.

A DOMESTIC POEM FOR PORTIA

This is all it is.
These pictures cast up in front of me
with the mind's various energies.
Hence so many flies in this old granary.
I've become one of those blackened beef sides
hanging in a South American market so when I sing
to myself I dispel a black cloud around my mouth
and when Linda brings iced tea she thinks I'm only
a photo in the *National Geographic* and drinks the tea
herself, musing he's snuck off to the bar
and his five year pool game.
This seems to be all it is.
Garcia sings "brown eyed women and red grenadine."
Some mother source of pleasure so that the guitar
mutes and revolves the vision of her as she rinses
her hair bending thigh deep in the lake, her buttocks appear
to be struggling by themselves to get out of that bikini
with a faint glisten of sun at each cheek top.
But when I talked to her she was thin in the head,
a magazine photo slipping through the air like
a stringless kite.
It's apparent now that this is all there is.
This shabby wicker chair, music, the three P.M.
glass of red wine as a reward for sitting still
as our parents once instructed us. "Sit still!"
I want my head to go visit friends, traveling they call it
and without airports. Then little Anna up to her neck
in the lake for the first time, the ancient lineage
of swimming revealing itself in her two year old fat
body, eyes sparkle with awe and delight in this natural
house of water. Hearing a screech I step to the porch
and see three hawks above the neighbor's pasture
chasing each other in battle or courtship.
This must be all there is.
At full rest with female wet eyes becoming red wondering
falsely how in christ's name am I going to earn
enough to keep us up in the country where the air

is sweet and green, an immense kingdom of water nearby
and five animals looking to me for food, and two daughters
and a mother assuming my strength. I courageously fix
the fence, mulch the tomatoes, fertilize the pasture—
a nickel-plated farmer. Wake up in the middle
of the night frightened, thinking nearly two decades
ago I took my vows and never dreamed I'd be responsible
for so many souls. Eight of them whispering provide.
This could very well be all that there is.
And I'm not unhappy with it. A check in the mail that will
take us through another month. I see in the papers
I've earned us "lower class"! How strange. Waiting
for Rachel's foal to drop. That will make nine. Provide.
Count my big belly ten. But there's an odd grace in being
an ordinary artist. A single tradition clipping the heads
off so many centuries. Those two drunks a millennia ago on
a mountaintop in China—laughing over the beauty of the moment.
At peace despite their muddled brains. The male dog, a trifle
stupid, rushes through the door announcing absolutely nothing.
He has great confidence in me. I'm hanging on to nothing today and
with confidence, a sureness that the very air between our bodies,
the light of what we are, has to be enough.

MISSY 1966–1971

I want to be worthy of this waking dream—
    floating   above
    the August landscape
in a coffin with my dog
who's just died from fibroid cancer.
Yes. We'll be up there and absorb
the light of stars and phosphorus
like the new Army telescopic sights
and the light hanging captive
in clouds
and the light glittering upward
from the water
and porchlights
from the few trucks & cars
at 3 A.M.
and one lone airliner.
Grief holding us safe in a knot we'll float
over every mile we covered, birch clump, thorn apple,
wild cherry trees and aspen in search of grouse,
your singular white figure fixed then as Sirius the Dog Star.
I think this crazed boy striking
out at nothing
wants to join you
so homeward
bound.

from

RETURNING
TO EARTH

RETURNING TO EARTH

for Guy and Anna

She
pulls the sheet of this dance
across me
then runs, staking
the corners far out at sea.

* * *

So curious in the middle of America, the only "locus"
I know, to live and love at great distance. (Growing
up, everyone is willing to drive seventy miles to see
a really big grain elevator, ninety miles for a dance,
two hundred to look over a pair of Belgian mares
returning the next day for the purchase, three hundred
miles to see Hal Newhouser pitch in Detroit, eight
hundred miles to see the Grand Ole Opry, a thousand
miles to take the mongoloid kid to a Georgia faith healer.)
I hitched two thousand for my first glimpse of the Pacific.
When she first saw the Atlantic she said near Key Largo
"I thought it would be bigger."

* * *

I widowed my small
collection of magic
until it poisoned itself with longing.
I have learned nothing.
I give orders to the rain.
I tried to catch the tempest in a gill net.
The stars seem a little closer lately.
I'm no longer afraid to die
but is this a guidepost of lunacy?
I intend to see the 10 hundred million worlds Manjusri
passed through before he failed to awaken the maiden.

Taking off and landing are the dangerous times.
I was commanded in a dream to dance.

* * *

O Faustus talks to himself,
talks to himself, talks to himself,
talks to himself, talks to himself,
Faustus talks to himself,
talks to himself.

* * *

Ikkyu's ten years near the whorehouses
shortens distances, is truly palpable;
and in ten years you will surely
get over your itch. Or not.

* * *

Don't waste yourself staring at the moon.
All of those moon-staring-rear-view-mirror deaths!
Study the shadow of the horse turd in the grass.
There must be a difference between looking at a picture
of a bird and the actual bird (barn swallow)
fifteen feet from my nose on the shed eaves.
That cloud SSW looks like the underside
of a river in the sky.

* * *

O I'm lucky
got a car that starts almost every day
tho' I want a new yellow Chevy pickup
got two letters today
and I'd rather have three
have a lovely wife
but want all the pretty ones
got three white hawks in the barn
but want a Himalayan eagle

[166]

have a planet in the basement
but would prefer the moon in the granary
have the northern lights
but want the Southern Cross.

* * *

The stillness of this earth
which we pass through
with the precise speed of our dreams.

* * *

I'm getting very old. If I were a mutt
in dog years I'd be seven, not stray so far.
I am large. Tarpon my age are often large
but they are inescapably fish. A porpoise
my age was the King of New Guinea in 1343.
Perhaps I am king of my dogs, cats, horses,
but I have dropped any notion of explaining
to them why I read so much. To be mysterious
is a prerogative of kingship. I discovered
lately that my subjects do not live a life,
but are life itself. They do not recognize
the pain of the schizophrenia of kingship.
To them I am pretty much a fellow creature.

* * *

So distances: yearns for Guyaquil and Petersburg,
the obvious Paris and Rome,
restraint in the Cotswolds, perfumes of Arusha,
Entebbe bristling with machine guns,
also Ecuadorian & Ethiopian airports,
border guards always whistling in boredom
and playing with machine guns;
all to count the flies on the lion's eyelids
and the lioness hobbling in deep grass
lacking one paw, to scan the marlin's caudal fin
cutting the Humboldt swell, an impossible scissors.

* * *

There must be a cricket named Zagreus
in the granary tucked under a roof beam,
under which my three year old daughter
boogies madly,
her first taste of the Grateful Dead;
she is well out of her mind.

* * *

Rain on the tin roof which covers a temple,
rain on my walking head which covers a temple,
rain covering my laugh shooting
towards the woods for no reason,
rain splattering in pasture's heat
raising cones of dust,
and off the horses' backs,
on oriole's nest in ash tree,
on my feet poking out the door,
testing the endurance of our actual pains,
biting hard against the sore tooth.

* * *

She's rolling in the bear fat
She's rolling in the sand
She's climbing a vine
She's boarding a jet
She flies into the distance wearing blue shoes

* * *

Having become the person I most feared in Childhood—
A DRUNKARD. They were pointed out to us
in our small town: oil workers, some poor farmers,
on Saturday marketing, a mechanic, a fired teacher.
They'd stumble when walking, sometimes yell
on the street at noon, wreck their old cars;
their wives would request special prayers in church,

and the children often came to school in winter
with no socks. We took up a collection to buy
the dump-picker's daughter shoes. Also my uncles
are prone to booze, also my father though it was well
controlled, and now my fifteen-year war with the bottle
with whiskey removing me from the present
in a sweet, laughing haze, removing anger, anxiety,
instilling soft grandness, decorating ugliness
and reaffirming my questionable worth. SEE: Olson's
fingers touch his thumb, encircling the bottle—he
gulps deeply, talking through one night into the next
afternoon, talking, basking in Gorton's fishy odor.
So many of my brethren seem to die of busted guts.
Now there is a measured truce with maps and lines
drawn elegantly against the binge, concessions,
measurings, hesitant steps. My favorite two bars
are just north and barely south of the 45th parallel.

* * *

I no longer believe in the idea of magic,
christs, the self, metal buddhas, bibles.
A horse is only the space his horseness requires.
If I pissed in the woods would a tree see my ear
fall off and would the ear return to the body
on the morning of the third day? Do Bo trees
ever remember the buddhas who've slept beneath them?
I admit that yesterday I built an exploratory altar.
Who can squash his delight in incomprehension?
So on a piece of old newspaper I put an earthworm
on a maple leaf, the remains of a bluebird after
the cat was finished—head and feet, some dog hair,
shavings from when we trimmed the horses' hoofs,
a snakeskin, a stalk of ragweed, a gourd,
a lemon, a cedar splinter, a nonsymbolic doorknob,
a bumblebee with his juice sucked out by a wasp.
Before this altar I invented a doggerel mantra
it is this   it is this   it is this

* * *

It is very hard to give birds advice.
They are already members of eternity.
In their genes they have both compass
and calendar. Their wing bones are hollow.
We are surprised by how light a dead bird is.

* * *

But what am I penetrating?
Only that it seems nothing convinces
itself or anyone else reliably
of its presence. It is in the distance.

* * *

No Persephone in my life,
Ariadne, Helen, Pocahontas,
Evangeline of the Book House
but others not less extraordinary who step
lightly into the dream life, refusing to leave:
girl in a green dress,
woman lolling in foot deep Caribbean,
woman on balcony near Vatican,
girl floating across Copley Square in 1958,
mythologized woman in hut in 1951,
girl weeping in lilacs,
woman slapping my face,
girl smoking joint in bathtub looking at big toe,
slender woman eating three lobsters,
woman who blew out her heart with cocaine,
girl livid and deformed in dreams,
girl breaking the window in rage,
woman sick in hotel room,
heartless woman in photo—
not heartless but a photo.

* * *

My left eye is nearly blind.
No words have ever been read with it.
Not that the eye is virgin—thirty years ago

it was punctured by glass. In everything
it sees a pastel mist. The poster of Chief Joseph
could be King Kong, Hong Kong, a naked lady riding
a donkey into Salinas, Kansas. A war atrocity.
This eye is the perfect art critic. This eye
is a perfect lover saying bodies don't matter,
it is the voice. This eye can make a lightbulb
into the moon when it chooses. Once a year I open
it to the full moon out in the pasture and yell
white light white light.

* * *

A half dozen times a day
I climb through the electric fence
on my way and back to my study
in the barnyard. I have to be cautious.
I have learned my true dimensions,
how far my body sticks out from my brain.

* * *

We are each
the only world
we are going to get.

* * *

I don't want to die. It would certainly
inconvenience my wife and daughters.
I am sufficiently young that it would help
my publisher unpack his warehouse of books.
It would help me stop drinking and lose weight.
I could talk to Boris Pasternak.
He never saw the film.

* * *

Wanting to pull the particular nail
that will collapse the entire house
so that there is nothing there,

not even a foundation, a rubble heap,
no sign at all, just grass, weeds and trees
among which you cannot find a shard of masonry
which like an arrowhead, might suggest
an entire civilization.

* * *

She was lying back in the rowboat.
It was hot.
She tickled me with her toes.
She picked lily pads.
She watched mating dragonflies.
"How many fish below us?"
"O a hundred or so."
"It would be fun to fall in love with someone."
The rower continued his rowing.

* * *

Why be afraid of a process you're
already able to describe with precision?
To say you don't believe in it
is to say that you're *not.*
It doesn't care so why should you?
You've been given your body back
without a quarrel. See this vision
of your imagined body float toward you:
it disappears into you without a trace.
You feel full with a fullness again.
Your dimensions aren't scattered in dreams.

* * *

This fat pet bird I've kept so many years,
a crow with a malformed wing
tucked against its side, no doubt a vestigial fin:
I taught him early to drink from my whiskey
or wine glass in the shed but he prefers wine.
He flies only in circles of course
but when he drinks he flies in great

circles miles wide, preferring bad days
with low cold clouds looking like leper brains.
I barely hear his wimps & howls: O jesus
the pain O shit it hurts O god let it end.
He drags himself through air mostly landing
near a screen door slamming, a baby's cry,
a dog's bark, a forest fire, a sleeping coyote.
These fabulous memories of earth!

* * *

Not to live in fancy
these short hours: let shadows
fall from walls as shadows, nothing else.
New York is exactly
dead center
in New York.
Not to indulge this heartsickness as failure.
Did I write three songs or seven
or half a one, one line, phrases?
A single word
that might hang in the still, black air
for more than a few moments?
Then the laughter comes again.
We *sing it away.*
What short wicks
we fuel with our blood.

* * *

Disease!
My prostate beating & pulsing
down there like a frightened turkey's heart.

* * *

A cold day,
low ceiling.
A cloud the size
of a Greyhound bus
just hit the house.

* * *

Offenses this summer against Nature:
poured iced tea on a garter snake's head
as he or she dozed on the elm stump,
pissed on a bumblebee (inattentive),
kicked a thousand wasps to death in my slippers.
Favors done this summer for Nature:
let the mice keep their nest in the green station wagon,
let Rachel the mare breathe her hot damp horse breath
against my bare knee when she wanted to,
tried without success to get the song sparrow out
of the shed where she had trapped herself fluttering
along the cranny under the assumption that the way *out*
is always the way *up,* and her wings lie to her
with each separate beat against the ceiling saying
there is no way down and out,
there is no way down and out,
the open door back into the world.

* * *

Coleridge's pet spider
he says is very intellectual,
spins webs of deceit
straight out of his big
hanging ass.

* * *

Mandrill, *Mandrillus sphinx,*
crest, mane, beard, yellow, purple, green
a large fierce, gregarious baboon
has small wit but ties himself to a typewriter
with wolfish and bloody appetite.
He is just one, thousands will follow,
something true to be found among the countless
millions of typed pages. There's a picture
of him in Tibet though no mandrills have been known
to live there. He wants to be with his picture
though there's no way to get there. So he types.

[174]

So he dreams *lupanar lupanar lupanar*
brothels with steam and white dust, music
that describes undiscovered constellations
so precisely the astronomers of the next century
will know where to look. Peaches dripping light.
Lupanar. The female arriving in dreams is unique,
not another like her on earth; she's created for a moment.
It only happens one time. One time O one time.
He types. She's his only real food.
O *lupanar* of dreams.

* * *

Head bobbing right and left,
with no effort
and for the first time
I see all sides of the pillar at once,
the earth,   her body.

* * *

I can't jump
high anymore.

* * *

He tightens
pumps in blue cold air
gasoline
the electricity from summer storms
the seven by seven foot
blue face of lightning
that shot down the gravel road
like a ghost rocket.

* * *

Saw the lord of crows
late at night in my living room;
don't know what true color of man—
black-white-red-yellow—

as he was hooded with the mask of a crow;
arms, legs, with primary feathers sewn to leather
downy black breast
silver bells at wrist
long feathered tail
dancing for a moment or two then disappearing.
Only in the morning did it occur to me
that it was a woman.

* * *

What sways us is not each other
but our dumb insistent pulse beating
I was I am I will I was
sometimes operatic, then in church
or barroom tenor, drunkenly, in prayer,
slowly in the confusion of dreams
but the same tripartite, the three
of being here trailing off into itself,
no finale any more than a beginning
until all of us lie buried
in the stupefying ache of caskets.

* * *

This earth of intentions.
Moonfucked, you can't eat or drink
or sleep at ten feet. Kneeling, love
is at nose tip. Or wound about
each other our eyes forget that they are eyes
and begin to see. You remember individual
fence posts, fish, trees, ankles,
from your tenth year.
Those savages lacking other immediate alternatives
screwed the ground to exhaustion.

* * *

Bad art: walking away untouched, unmoving,
barely tickled, *amused,* diverted, killing time,
throwing salt on the grass. The grace of Yukio Mishima's

suicide intervening in the false harmony,
Kawabata decides to live longer, also a harmony.
In bad music, the cheapest and easiest way to get
out of it infers Clapton. Eros girdled in metal
and ozone. A man in a vacuum of images, stirring
his skull with his dick, sparing himself his future,
fancy bound, unparticular, unpeculiar, following
the strings of his dreaming to more dreaming
in a sump narcosis, never having given himself
over to his life, never owning an instant.

                              * * *

Week's eating log:
whitefish poached with lemon, onion, wine, garlic;
Chulapa—pork roasted twelve hours with pinto beans,
red peppers, chili powder; grilled twenty-two pounds
of beef ribs for friends; a lamb leg pasted with Dijon
mustard, soy, garlic; Chinese pork ribs; menudo
just for Benny & me as no one else would eat it—
had to cook tripe five hours then mix with hominy
and peppers with chorizo tacos on the side;
copious fresh vegetables, burgundy, columbard, booze
with all of the above; at night fevered dreams
of her sumptuous butt, a Mercator projection,
the map of an enormous meal in my brain.
Still trying to lose weight.

                              * * *

How strange to see a horse
stare
straight up.

                              * * *

Everything is a good idea at the time.
Staring with stupid longing at a picture, dumb struck
as they used to call it, an instant's whimsy;
a body needlessly unlike any others,
deserved by someone so monstrous

as Lucrezia Borgia: how do you come to terms
with it? thinks the American. You don't, *terms*
being a financial word not applicable
to bodies. Wisdom shies away, the packhorse
startled at the diamondback beneath the mesquite,
the beauty of threat. Now look at her as surely
as that other beast, the dead crow beneath the apple
tree so beautiful in its black glossiness
but without eyes, feet stiff and cool as the air.
I watched it for a year and owned its bleached
shinbone but gave it to someone who needed
the shinbone of a crow.

* * *

She says it's too hot,
the night's too short,
that I'm too drunk,
but it's not *too* anything, ever.

* * *

Living all my life with a totally normal-sized dick
(cf. the authorities, Van Velde, Masters & Johnson)
neither hedgehog or horse, neither emu or elephant
(saw one in Kenya, the girls said o my goodness)
neither wharf rat, arrogant buck dinosaur,
prepotent swan, ground squirrel, Lauxmont Admiral
famous holstein bull who sired 200,000 artificially.
I am saved from trying to punish anyone,
from confusing it with a gun, harpoon, cannon, sword,
cudgel, Louisville Slugger. It just sits there
in the dark, shy and friendly
like the new kid at school.

* * *

In our poetry we want to rub our nose hard
into whatever is before it; to purge
these dreams of pictures, photos, phantom people.

[178]

She offers a flex of butt, belly button, breasts,
slight puff of veneris, gap in teeth often capped,
grace of knees, high cheekbones and neck,
all the thickness of paper. The grandest illusion
as in ten thousand movies in all those hours
of dark, the only true sound the exploding
popcorn and the dairy fetor of butter. After the movie
a stack of magazines at the drugstore
to filter through, to be filtered through.

* * *

A choral piece for a dead dog:
how real the orchestra and hundred
voices on my lawn; pagan with the dog
on a high cedar platform to give the fire
its full marriage of air; the chorus
sings DOG a thousands times, dancing
in a circle. That would be a proper
dog funeral. By god. No dreams here
but a mighty shouting of dog.

* * *

Sunday night,
I'm lucky to have all of this vodka,
a gift of Stolichnaya.
And books. And a radio
playing WSM all the way from Nashville.
Four new pups in the bedroom.
The house snores. My tooth aches.
It is time to fry an egg.

* * *

Heard the fog horn out at sea,
saw horses' backs shiny with rain,
felt my belly jiggle as I walked
through the barnyard in a light rain
with my daughter's small red umbrella

to protect the not very precious manuscript,
tiptoeing barefoot in the tall wet grass
trying to avoid the snakes.

* * *

With all this rain
the pond is full.
The ducks are one week old
and already speak their language perfectly—
a soft nasal hiss.
With no instructions they skim bugs from the pond's
surface and look fearfully at me.

* * *

The minister whacks off as does the insurance man,
habitual golfer, sweet lady in her bower,
as do novelists, monks, nuns in nunneries,
maidens in dormitories, stallion against fence post,
goat against puzzled pig who does not cease feeding,
and so do senators, generals, wives during TV
game shows, movie stars and football players, students
to utter distraction, teachers, butchers, world leaders,
everyone except poets who fear the dreaded
growth of hair on the palms, blindness.
They know that even in an empty hotel room
in South Dakota that someone is watching.

* * *

With my dog
I watched a single crow
fly across the field.
We are each one.

* * *

Thirty feet up in the air
near the top of my novel I want a bird to sing
from the crown of the barn roof.

A hundred feet away there is a grove of trees,
maple and elm and ash,
placed quite accidentally before any of us were born.
Everyone remembers who planted the lilacs
forty years and three wars ago.

* * *

In the morning paper
the arsonist
who was also a paranoid schizophrenic,
a homosexual,
retarded,
an alcoholic
who lacerated his body with a penknife
and most significantly for the rest of us,
started fires where none were desired,
on whim.

* * *

Spent months regathering dreams lost in the diaspora,
all of the prism's colors, birds, animals, bodies,
getting them back within the skin
where they'd do no damage.
How difficult catching them armed
only with a butterfly catcher's net,
a gun, airplane, an ice pick,
a chalice of rainwater, a green headless
buddha on loan from a veteran of foreign wars.

* * *

Saw that third eye in a dream
but couldn't remember if it looked
from a hole in a wall of ice,
or a hole in a floor of ice,
but it was an eye looking from a hole in ice.

* * *

Two white-faced cattle out in the dark green pasture,
one in the shade of the woodlot,
one out in the hot sunlight,
eating slowly and staring at each other.

* * *

So exhausted after my walk from orchestrating
the moves of one billion August grasshoppers
plus fifty thousand butterflies
swimming at the heads
of fifty thousand wild flowers
red blue yellow orange
orange flowers the only things that rhyme with orange
the one rabbit in the pasture
one fly buzzing at the window
a single hot wind through the window
a man sitting at my desk resembling me.

* * *

He sneaks up on the temple slowly at noon.
He's so slow it seems like it's taking years.
Now his hands are on a pillar, the fingers
encircling it, with only the tips inside the gate.

* * *

After all of this long moist dreaming
I perceive how accurate the rooster's crow
is from down the road.

* * *

You can suffer and not even know you're suffering
because you've been suffering so long you can't remember
another life. You're actually a dead dog on a country road.
And a man gets used to his rotten foot.
After a while it's simply a rotten foot,
and his rotten ideas are even easier to get used to

because they don't hurt as much as a rotten foot.
The road from Belsen to Watergate paved
with perfectly comfortable ideas, ideas to sleep on
like a mattress stuffed with money and death,
an actual waterbed filled with liquid gold.
So our inept tuna cravings and Japan's (she imitates
our foulest features) cost an annual
250,000 particular dolphin deaths,
certainly as dear as people to themselves
or so the evidence says.

* * *

Near my lover's old frame house with a field
behind it, the grass is a brilliant gold.
Standing on the gravel road before the house
a great flock of blackbirds coming over so close
to my head I see them all individually,
eyes, crests, the feet drawn out in flight.

* * *

I owe the dentist nine hundred dollars.
This is more than I made on three
of my books of poems. But then I am gloriously
free. I can let my mouth rot and quit
writing poems. I could let the dentist
write the poems while I walked into the dark
with a tray of golden teeth I'd sculpt
for myself in the forms of shark's teeth,
lion's teeth, teeth of grizzly and python.
Watch me open my mouth as I wear these wondrous
teeth. The audience gross is exactly nine hundred!
The house lights dim. My lips part.
There is a glimpse of sun.

* * *

Abel always votes.
Cain usually thinks better of it

knowing not very deep in his heart
that no one deserves to be encouraged.
Abel has a good job & is a responsible screw,
but many intelligent women seem drawn
to Crazy Horse, a descendant of Cain,
even if he only gets off his buffalo pony
once a year to throw stones at the moon.
Of course these women marry Abel but at bars and parties
they are the first to turn to the opening door
to see who is coming in.

* * *

I was standing near the mow door
in the darkness, a party going on in the château.
She was there with her sister.
We kissed then lay down on fresh straw in a paddock.
An angry stallion jumped over on top of us.
I could see his outline clearly against the sky.
Why did we die so long ago.

* * *

How wind, cloud and water
blaspheme symmetry at every instant,
forms that can't be remembered and stored:
Grand Marais, Cape Ann at Eastern Point,
Lake Manyara from a cliff, Boca Grande's sharks
giving still water a moving shape—they are there
and there and there—the waterfall next to a girl
so obviously on a white horse, to mud
puddle cat avoids, back to Halibut Point,
Manitou convulsed in storms to thousand mile
weed line in Sargasso Sea to brown violent confluence
of Orinoco and ocean off Devil's Gate; mixing wind,
cloud, water, the purest mathematics of their
description studied as glyphs, alchemists
everywhere working with humble gold, somewhere to begin,
having to keep eyes closed to wind, cloud, water.

* * *

Saw an ox. A black horse I recognized.
A procession of carts full of flowers
pulled by nothing. Asymmetrical planets.
Fish out of their element of water.
Simple music—a single note an hour.
How are we to hear it, if at all?
No music in statement, the lowest denominator
by which our fragments can't find each other.
But I can still hear the notes of April,
the strained, fragile notes of March:
convalescent, tentative, a weak drink
taken over and over in immense doses.
It is the body that is the suite entire,
brain firmly fused to the trunk, spine
more actual than mountains, brain moving
as a river, governed precisely by her energies.

* * *

Whippoorwill. Mourning dove. Hot morning rain
changing to a violent squall coming SSW out of the lake,
thunder enveloping itself then unfolding
as cloth in wind furls, holds back, furls again;
running nearly naked in shorts to my shed,
thunder rattling windows and walls,
acorns rattling against barn's tin roof;
the floor shudders, then stillness as squall passes,
as strange as a strong wind at summer twilight
when the air is yellow. Now cool still air.
Mourning dove.
Oriole.

* * *

O my darling sister
O she crossed over
she's crossed over
is planted now near her father
six feet under earth's skin—
their still point on this whirling earth
now and I think forever.

* * *

Now it is as close to you as the clothes you wear.
The clothes are attached to your body
by a cord that runs up your spine, out your neck
and through the earth, back up your spine.

* * *

At nineteen I began to degenerate,
slight smell of death in my gestures,
unbelieving, tentative, wailing . . .
so nineteen years have gone. It doesn't matter.
It might have taken fifty. Or never.
Now the barriers are dissolving, the stone fences
in shambles. I want to have my life
in cloud shapes, water shapes, wind shapes,
crow call, marsh hawk swooping over grass and weed tips.
Let the scavenger take what he finds.
Let the predator love his prey.

NEW POEMS

NOT WRITING MY NAME

In the snow, that is. The "J" could have been
three hundred yards into the high pasture
across the road. The same with the "I" which I intended
to dot by sprawling and flopping in a drift. The "M"
naturally would have required something more
than twelve hundred yards of hard walking as we
have two empty-bottomed isosceleses to deal with.
What star-crossed jock ego would churn through those
drifts to write a name invisible except to crows?
And the dog would have confused the crows the way
he first runs ahead, then criss-crosses my path.
It's too cold anyhow—ten below at noon though the sun
would tell me otherwise. And the wind whips coils
and wisps of snow across the hardened drifts and around
my feet like huge ghost snakes. These other signatures:
vole tracks so light I have to kneel to trace his
circlings which are his name. Vole. And an unknown bird,
scarcely heavier than the vole, that lacks a left foot. Fox tracks
leading up a drift onto my favorite boulder where he swished
his tail, definitely peed, and left. The dog sniffs
the tracks, also pees but sparingly. He might need it later,
he saves his messages. For a moment mastodons float
through the trees, thunderhead colored, stuffing their maws
with branches. This place used to be Africa. Now it's so cold
there are blue shadows in my footprints, and a blue shadow
dog runs next to my own, flat and rippling to the snow, less than
paper thick. I try to invoke a crow for company; none appears.
I have become the place the crow didn't appear.

FROG

First memory
of swimming underwater:
eggs of frogs hanging in diaphanous clumps
from green lily pad stems;
at night in the tent I heard
the father of it all booming
and croaking in the reeds.

ROOSTER

to Pat Ryan

I have to kill the rooster tomorrow. He's being an asshole,
having seriously wounded one of our two hens with his insistent banging.
You walk into the barn to feed the horses and pick up an egg
or two for breakfast and he jumps her proclaiming she's mine she's mine.
Her wing is torn and the primary feathers won't grow back.
Chickens have largely been denatured, you know. He has no part
in those delicious fresh eggs. He crows on in a vacuum. He is
utterly pointless. He's as dumb as a tapeworm and no one cares
if he lives or dies. There. I can kill him
with an easy mind. But I'm still not up to it. Maybe I can hire
a weasel or a barn rat to do the job, or throw him to Justine,
the dog, who would be glad to rend him except the neighbors
have chickens too, she'd get the habit and we would have a beloved shot
dog to bury. So he deserves to die, having no purpose. We'll
have stewed barnyard chicken, closer to eating a gamebird than
that tasteless supermarket chicken born and bred in a caged
darkness. Everything we eat is dead except an occasional oyster
or clam. Should I hire the neighbor boy to kill him? Will the
hens stop laying out of grief? Isn't his long wavering crow
magnificent? Isn't the worthless rooster the poet's bird brother?
No. He's just a rooster and the world has no place for him.
Should I wait for a full wintry moon, take him to the top of the
hill after dropping three hits of mescaline and strangle him?
Should I set him free for a fox meal? They're coming back now
after the mange nearly wiped them out. He's like a leaking roof
with drops falling on my chest. He's the Chinese torture in the barn.
He's lust mad. His crow penetrates walls. His head bobs in lunar
jerks. The hens shudder but are bored with the pain of eggs.
What can I do with him? Nothing isn't enough. In the morning
we will sit down together and talk it out. I will tell him he
doesn't matter and he will wag his head, strut, perhaps crow.

EPITHALAMIUM

for Peter and Maria

For the first time the wind
blew straight down from the heavens.
I was wandering around the barnyard
about three A.M. in full moonlight
when it started, flattening my hair
against my head; my dog cowered
between my knees, and the last leaves
of a cold November shot to the ground.
Then the wind slowed and went back to the north.
This happened last night and already at noon
my faith in it is passing.

A REDOLENCE FOR NIMS

O triple sob—turned forty
at midnight—body at dawn
booze-soddened but hopeful,
knowing that the only thing
to remember is dreams.
Dead clear zero, Sunday afternoon
in an attic of a closed resort
on Lake Michigan with one lone
duck riding the diminishing
swells of yesterday's storm
against the snowy cliffs of North Manitou:
Who are we to love?
How many and what for?
My heart's gone to sea for years.
This is a prayer, plaint, wish,
howl of void beneath breastbone.
Dreams, soul chasers, bring
back my heart alive.

FOLLOWERS

Driving east on buddha's birthday,
April 9, 1978, past my own birthplace
Grayling, Michigan, south 300 miles to Toledo,
then east again to New York for no reason—
belled heart swinging in grief for months
until I wanted to take my life in my hands;
three crows from home followed above
the car until the Delaware River where
they turned back: one stood all black
and lordly on a fresh pheasant killed
by a car: all this time
counting the mind, counting crows,
each day's ingredients
the same, barring rare
bad luck
good luck
dumb luck
all set in marble by the habitual,
locked as the day passes moment by moment:
say on the tracks the train can't
turn 90 degrees to the right because it's not
the nature of a train,
but we think a man can dive
in a pond, swim across it,
and climb a tree though few of us do.

MY FIRST DAY AS A PAINTER

Things to paint:
my dog (yellow),
nude women,
dead coyote with grey whiskers,
nude women,
a tree full of crows,
nude women,
the self in the mirror,
nude women,
a favorite cloud,
nude women,
a worn out scalpel,
nude women,
dead friends,
nude women ages 14–80 (12–82),
call me wherever you are at noon
in the glory of noon light,
bring your dogs and birds,
everybody is welcome:
Nude women spinning in godlike whirls
creating each other in endless
streams of human eggs!

WAITING

There are no calls from the outside.
Miracles are the perversity of literature.
We should know that by now.
Only that these never revealed connections of things
lead us oddly on. Caesar's legions
entering Greenland's ice, the scout far in front
wanting to do battle where there are
no enemies,
never were any enemies.

NOON

Spring: despondency,
fall: despair,
onset of winter
a light rain in the heart
the pony tethered to the telephone
pole day after day until he's eaten
the circle, moved to another pole,
another circle: winter never deepens
but falls dead upon the ground,
body of the sky whirled
in grey gusts:
from Manitoba stretched brains
of north; heat for heart, head,
in smallest things—dry socks,
strange breasts, an ounce of sun
glittering above the blue shadows
of the barn.

BIRTHDAY

The masques of dream—monk in his
lineage—what does he wear to shield
himself? First shield made of a cloud,
second—a tree, third—a shadow; and
leading to the stretched coils of light
(how they want to gather us up
with our permission) three men.
Two dead tho' dead is supernumerary.
The cause is the effect.
He laughed like a lake would
but only once, never twice into the same
mystery. Not ever to stop but only
to drop the baggage, to shed the
39th skin.

CLEAR WATER 3

Ah, yes. Fame never got anyone
off the hook, it seems. Some poignant
evidence to be offered here in McGuane.
There's a cutoff beyond which a certain
number of people know you exist for various
reasons, good or bad or with a notorious
indifference.   Said Spicer:
My vocabulary did this to me. Meaning
what he was, near death in an alcoholic ward.
Crane or Cavafy. Alcohol as biography
more surely than serial poems. I doubt it.
We are drawn to where we end like water
for reasons of character, volume, gravity,
the sound we make in passing/ not all the sounds
we made in passing in one place—a book.
Each day's momentum of voice carrying
backwards and forwards to the limits, beginning
and end. We drink to enchant our voices,
to heal them, to soothe with laughter, to glide
awhile. My words kill, killed, me, my lord. Yes.

DOGEN'S DREAM

What happens when the god of spring
meets spring? He thinks for a moment
of great whales travelling from the bottom
to the top of the earth, the day the voyage
began seven million years ago
when spring last changed its season.
He enters himself, emptiness
desiring emptiness. He sleeps
and his sleep is the dance of all the birds
on earth flying north.

WEEPING

Six days of clouds since
I returned from Montana,
a state of mind out West.
A bleak afternoon in the granary killing flies and wasps.
Sitting on a *zafu* watching flies.
Two days ago a sandhill crane flew over
so low I could see an eyeball clearly cocked
toward my singular own.
As I drink I miss more flies.
I am searching out the ecstatic life
with fly swatter and wine glass in hand,
the sky above an inverted steel sink.
I am looking for weeping
which is a superior form of rest.
Can't there be dry weeping? Nope.
Dry weeping is like dry fucking
which most of us remember as unsatisfying.
Wet fucking is another story
but not the object here, though decidedly
more interesting than weeping.
I would frankly like to throw
myself around and have some real passion.
Some wet passion! to be sure.
At nineteen in 1957 on Grove Street in NY
I could weep about art, Hart Crane, my empty
stomach, homesickness for pheasants and goldenrod,
Yesenin's suicide, a red-haired girl with an improbable
butt, my dad planting the garden alone.
It was a year in which I wrung out pillowcases at dawn.
But this is the flip side of the record, a log
of the search for weeping. I've been dry
for a decade and it isn't panning out.
Like a Hollywood producer I sit by a pool
and hatch inane plots against the weeping imagination,
spinning wheels, treading water,
beating the mental bishop,
flogging the mental clam,

pulling the mental wire
like a cub scout in a lonely pup tent.
I'm told I laugh too much.
I laugh deeply at Johnny Carson monologues,
at my poetry, at health food & politics,
at the tragic poetry of others, at the weedy garden,
at my dog hitting the electric fence,
at women freeing themselves when I am in bondage,
at the thought of my death.
In fact I'm tickled pink with life.
I actually have a trick to weep but it's cheating.
I used it once when I was very drunk.
I thought of the deaths of my wife and daughters.
I threw myself to the floor weeping.
I wept horribly and shook, gnashed my teeth.
I must die before them.

THE CHATHAM GHAZAL

It is the lamp on the kitchen table
well after midnight saying nothing but light.

Here are a list of ten million measurements.
You may keep them. Or throw them away.

A strange warm day when November has forgotten
to be November. Birds form shrill clouds.

Phototropiques. We emerge upward from liquid.
See the invisible husks we've left behind called memories.

The press wonders how we drink so much poison and stay
alive. The antidote is chance, mobility, sleeplessness.

They've killed another cow. With the mountain of guts
I also bury all of the skins of thirty-seven years.

MARRIAGE GHAZAL

for Peter & Beck

Hammering & drifting. Sea wrack. Cast upon & cast out.
Who's here but shore? Where we stop is where shore is.

I saw the light beyond mountains turned umber by morning.
I walked by memory as if I had no legs. Or head.

In a bed of reeds I found my body and entered it,
taking my life upon myself, the soul made comfortable.

So the body's a nest for the soul and we set out inland,
the figure of a walker who only recognized the sea and moon.

And coming to the first town the body became a chorus—
O my god this is a place or thing and I'll stay awhile.

The body met a human with fur and the moon mounted her head
in an arc when she sat & they built a boat together.

MARCH WALK

I was walking because I wasn't upstairs sitting.
I could have been looking for pre-1900 gold coins
in the woods all afternoon. What a way to make a living!
The same mastodon was there only three hundred yards from
where I last saw him. I felt the sabers on the saber tooth,
the hot wet breath on the back of my hand. Three deer
and a number of crows, how many will remain undisclosed:
It wasn't six and it wasn't thirty. There were four girls
ranging back to 1957. The one before that just arrived
upstairs. There was that long morose trip into the world
hanging onto my skin for a quarter of a mile, shed with some
difficulty. There was one dog, my own, and one grouse
not my own. A strong wind flowed over and through us like
dry water. I kissed a scar on a hip. I found a rotting
crabapple and a distant relative to quartz. You could spend
a lifetime and still not walk to an island. I met none of the
dead today having released them yesterday at three o'clock.
If you're going to make love to a woman you have to give
her some of your heart. Else don't. If I had found a gold coin
I might have left it there with my intermittent interest in
money. The dead snipe wasn't in the same place but the rocks
were. The apple tree was a good place to stand. Every late fall
the deer come there for dessert. They will stand for days
waiting for a single apple to tumble from the upmost limb.

THE WOMAN FROM SPIRITWOOD

Sleeping from Mandan to Jamestown,
waking near Spiritwood in the van,
shrinking in fever with the van
buffeted by wind so that it shudders,
the wind maybe fifty knots straight N by NW
out of Saskatchewan. Stopping for gas we see men
at the picnic tables cleaning the geese they've shot:
October first with the feathers carried off by the wind
into fields where buffalo once roamed, also
the Ogalala & Miniconjou Sioux roamed in search
of buffalo and Crazy Horse on a horse that outlived him.
She comes out of the station, smiling, leaning into the wind.
She is so beautiful that an invisible hand reaches
into your rib cage and twists your heart one notch
counterclockwise. There is nowhere to go.
I've been everywhere and there's nowhere to go.
The talk is halting, slow until it becomes
the end of another part of the future.
I scratch gravel toward and from this wound,
seeing within the shadow that this shadow casts
how freedom must be there
before there can be freedom.

GATHERING APRIL

for Simic

Stuffing a crow call in one ear
and an unknown bird's in the other,
laying on the warm cellar door out of
the cool wind which I take small sparing
bites of with three toes still wet from the pond's
edge: April is so violent up here you hide
in corners or when in the woods, in swales
and behind beech trees. Twenty years ago
this April I offered my stupid heart up to
this bloody voyage. It was near a marsh
on a long walk. You can't get rid of those
thousand pointless bottles of whiskey
that you brought along. Last night after
the poker game I read Obata's Li Po.
He was no less a fool but adding those
twenty thousand poems you come up
with a god. There are patents on all
the forms of cancer but still we praise
god from whom or which all blessings flow,
that an April exists, that a body lays itself
down on a warm cellar door and remembers, drinks
in birds and wind, whiskey, frog songs
from the marsh, the little dooms hiding
in the shadow of each fence post.

WALTER OF BATTERSEA

for Anjelica

I shall commit suicide or die
trying, Walter thought beside
the Thames—at low tide and very
feminine.

Picture him: a cold November day,
the world through a long lens; he's
in new blue pants and races the river
for 33 steps.

Walter won. Hands down. Then lost
again. Better to die trying! The sky
so bleak. God blows his nose above
the Chelsea Flour Mills.

What is he at 40, Nov. 9, 1978, so far
from home: grist for his own mill; all
things have become black and white
without hormonal surge.

And religious. He's forgiven god
for the one hundred ladies who turned him
down and took him up. O that song—
I asked her for water and she gave
me kerosene.

No visions of Albion, no visions at all,
in fact, the still point of the present winding
about itself, graceful, unsnarled. I am
here today and gone tomorrow.

How much is he here? Not quite with
all his heart and soul. Step lightly
or the earth revolves into a berserk
spin. Fall off or dance.

And choosing dance not god, at least
for the time being. Things aren't what

they seem but what they are—infinitely
inconsolable.

He knows it's irony that's least
valuable in this long death watch.
Irony scratching its tired ass. No trade-offs
with time and fortune.

It's indelicate to say things twice except
in prayer. The drunk repeats to keep
his grasp, a sort of prayer: the hysteria
of the mad a verbless prayer.

Walter recrossed the bridge which was
only a bridge. He heard his footsteps
just barely behind him. The river is not
where it starts and ends.

AFTER READING TAKAHASHI

for Lucien and Peter

Nothing is the same to anyone.
Moscow is east of Nairobi
but thinks of herself as perpetually west.
The bird sees the top of my head,
an even trade for her feathered belly.
Our eyes staring through the nose bridge
never to see each other.
She is not I, I not her.
So what, you think, having little
notion of my concerns. O that dank
basement of "so what" known by all
though never quite in the same way.
All of us drinking through a cold afternoon,
our eyes are on the mirror behind
the bottles, on the snow out the window
which the wind chases fruitlessly,
each in his separateness drinking,
talk noises coming out of our mouths.
In the corner a pretty girl plays pinball.
I have no language to talk to her.
I have come to the point in life when
I could be her father. This was never true before.
The bear hunter talked about the mountains.
We looked at them together out of the
tavern window in Emigrant, Montana.
He spent fifty years in the Absaroka Mountains
hunting grizzly bears and at one time, wolves.
We will never see the same mountains.
He knows them like his hands, his wife's
breasts and legs, his old dog sitting outside
in the pickup. I only see beautiful mountains
and say "beautiful mountains" to which he nods
graciously but they are a photo of China to me.
And all lessons are fatal: the great snowy owl
that flew in front of me so that

I ducked in the car; it will never happen again.
I've been warned by a snowy night, an owl,
the infinite black above and below me to look
at all creatures and things with a billion eyes,
not struggling with the single heartbeat
that is my life.